SHELL-SHOCK

Also by Anthony Babington

No Memorial

The Power to Silence
A History of Punishment in Britain

A House in Bow Street
Crime and the Magistracy, London 1740–1881

The English Bastille
A History of Newgate Gaol and Prison Conditions in Britain
1188–1902

The Rule of Law in Britain
From the Roman Occupation to the Present Day

For the Sake of Example
Capital Courts Martial 1914–1920

Military Intervention in Britain
From the Gordon Riots to the Gibraltar Incident

The Devil to Pay
The Mutiny of the Connaught Rangers in India, 1920

SHELL-SHOCK

A History of the Changing
Attitudes to War Neurosis

by
Anthony Babington

LEO COOPER
LONDON

First published in Great Britain in 1997 by
LEO COOPER
an imprint of
Pen & Sword Books Ltd
47 Church Street
Barnsley
South Yorkshire
S70 2AS

© Anthony Babington, 1997

ISBN 0 85052 562 4

A catalogue record for this book is
available from the British Library

Typeset by Phoenix Typesetting, Ilkley, West Yorkshire

Printed in England by Redwood Books, Trowbridge, Wiltshire

Survivors

No doubt they'll soon get well; the shock and strain
Have caused their stammering, disconnected talk.
Of course they're "longing to go out again," –
These boys with old, scared faces, learning to walk.
They'll soon forget their haunted nights; their cowed
Subjection to the ghosts of friends who died, –
Their dreams that drip with murder; and they'll be proud
Of glorious war that shatter'd all their pride . . .
Men who went out to battle, grim and glad;
Children, with eyes that hate you, broken and mad.

Siegfried Sassoon

Craiglockhart
October, 1917

Foreword

This is not a medical book. I am neither a doctor nor a psychologist. The book is essentially concerned with the adversities of ordinary soldiers – what was expected of them, what they endured and what happened to them after they had reached the limits of their fortitude.

For many years it was believed that soldiers on campaign were prone to certain strange, endemic maladies. These were given various names and were attributed to various causes. It was only fairly recently that it was realized that most of the disorders had a psychiatric origin.

I first encountered war neurosis while I was serving as an infantry officer during the Second World War and I saw men breaking down on the battlefield. Years later I was writing a book about capital courts martial in the 1914–1918 war and the Ministry of Defence granted me privileged access to the files relating to the trials of the condemned soldiers. On reading the evidence, I became convinced that some of the men had been suffering from what in those days was called "shell-shock" when they had committed the derelictions of duty for which they were executed. It was then I made up my mind that some day I would write a history of war neurosis and all of the misconceptions which had surrounded it in the past.

I should like to express my immense gratitude to my friend Robin Price, Librarian of The Wellcome Institute For The History Of Medicine, for the help and encouragement he gave me when I was carrying out my research, and to Claire Nutt, one of his assistants, who always managed to find for me the authorities I wished to read. I want, also, to mention my appreciation of the unfailing kindness which was shown to me by all the members of the staff at the Institute's library.

I am grateful as well to Tony McSeán, the Librarian of the British

Medical Association, and to Judithe Blacklaw, Librarian at the Whitehall Library of the Ministry of Defence, for supplying the photocopies of articles and documents which I required.

Finally, I wish to thank my niece Sally La Niece, for managing to read my handwriting and for preparing my manuscript for the publishers.

Anthony Babington

Chapter 1

On 12 March, 1915, Lance-Sergeant Walton, a 26-year-old soldier in the British Regular Army, was court-martialled for desertion. He was serving in the 2nd Battalion of the King's Royal Rifle Corps and in the middle of the previous August he had been among the first troops to arrive in France with the original British Expeditionary Force. His Division had engaged the leading formations of the advancing German Army outside the Belgian town of Mons on 22 August, and during the days that followed they had taken part in the arduous retreat which had continued without a pause until the Allies had managed to establish a defensive line to the south-east of Paris on 5 September. By then the BEF had trudged a distance of nearly two hundred miles, continuously harried by the enemy and suffering very heavy casualties. In the words of the Official History of the campaign, they had been "condemned at the very outset to undergo the severest ordeal which can be imposed on any army."[1] It was estimated that during the retreat the infantry had only had an average of four hours' rest a day; and when it had ended, according to a young officer in the BEF, the men had been physically weak from the long marches and mentally weak from the continual strain of always being within range of the German guns.[2]

Throughout the month of September the depleted Divisions of the BEF had been in constant action. At the beginning of October they had been moved from their positions east of Paris to take over the left sector of the Allied line, stretching southwards from the Channel Ports. From there they had immediately launched an offensive across the Flanders Plain in what became known as the First Battle of Ypres. Sergeant Walton's battalion was once again in the thick of the fighting.

On 29 October, when the BEF had been in hastily-prepared defensive positions round Ypres, the Germans had launched a massive attack on the town. Walton's Division was guarding the approaches to Gheluvelt, a strategically-important village on the road from Menin to Ypres, and had borne the brunt of the assault. The bitter struggle had lasted for four days during which Gheluvelt had changed hands three times. Eventually the British, heavily outnumbered and outgunned, had been forced to withdraw to a new line. All the battalions which had taken part in the action had suffered severe casualties.

At this stage, the Official History commented, the British Army "was composed of tired, haggard and unshaven men, unwashed, plastered with mud, many in little more than rags."[3]

The charge against Lance-Sergeant Walton was that he had deserted "near Ypres between the 1st and 9th November 1914", and that he had stayed at liberty until he was arrested by a French gendarme in a private house at Arques on 3 March, 1915. The details of his court martial are still retained in the Public Record Office at Kew.[4] He was tried by three officers, a Major, a Captain and a Lieutenant, and it is not disclosed whether or not he was represented by what was termed a "prisoner's friend". Usually a soldier on trial asked his platoon commander or his company commander to defend him.

The first witness for the prosecution was a sergeant from Walton's own battalion, who had seen him on duty with his company on 1 November and had heard later that he had been wounded and evacuated to hospital. The sergeant added at the end of his evidence that the battalion had been in action on the 1st and 2nd of November and had sustained heavy casualties on both days. On 9 November Walton had been reported "missing".

A crucial prosecution witness was a French civilian, a cobbler from Arques, a small village a few miles south of St Omer and about twenty-five miles from Ypres, who had first seen Walton in the vicinity of his house on the evening of 18 December. Walton was then without any arms or equipment; he looked cold and wet, had a bad cough and appeared to have been wounded in his left hand. The cobbler had taken sympathy on him and invited him to come in for a while and get warm by the fire. Walton had agreed to this proposal. Later he had asked if he could be put up for the night. The cobbler only had one bed in his home but he told Walton that he did not mind

4

sharing it with him. The arrangement had, in fact, continued for over two months. During this time, the cobbler said in his evidence, Walton had never tried to hide; he had drawn his rations from a neighbouring depot and he had frequently chatted to other British soldiers who happened to be in the village. Apart from one absence of five days, Walton had remained at the house until the day of his apprehension.

A gendarme gave formal evidence that, on 3 March, 1915, following a tip-off, he had visited the cobbler's house in Arques. He had found Walton there, wearing army uniform khaki trousers and a civilian jersey. The gendarme had arrested him as a suspected deserter.

On the following day Walton had made a written statement to the Military Police. He said that at the beginning of the previous November, during the fighting around Ypres, he had been detailed to collect some stragglers from other regiments. He had done this and had just taken them back to the front line when he was shot in the left hand. He had taken shelter in a trench to dress his wound and had remained there for several days before coming out to look for his battalion. His account continued in a somewhat rambling manner. He had found his way to Cassel, near St Omer, where he had reported to a French guard. Next he had been taken by car to see an English naval officer. Ever since then he had been walking about making enquiries, but he had been unable to find anyone who knew the whereabouts of the battalion. He concluded the statement by saying, "I am suffering from a nervous breakdown ever since I was wounded."

The day after Walton's arrest the Assistant Provost-Marshal for the Arques District had written a letter to the Commanding Officer of the 2nd Battalion of the King's Royal Rifle Corps, a copy of which was attached to the court-martial proceedings. Sergeant Walton, he said, "seems half-dazed and to be either unwilling to, or incapable of, giving straightforward answers to the simplest questions."

At his trial Walton gave evidence closely in accordance with his written statement to the Military Police. He had added that his reason for being in Arques was that he had been taken there by a naval officer who was trying to help him in locating his battalion. The court heard no medical witnesses for the prosecution or the defence and did not deem it advisable to adjourn so that further enquiries could be made. Apparently, Walton's contention that he had suffered a nervous

5

breakdown was either disbelieved or was not considered to be a valid defence, as he was convicted of the charge of desertion.

At that time a soldier on active service who had been found guilty of desertion could be sentenced to death, or to "such a lesser penalty as a court thought fit to impose".[5] The three officers who tried Sergeant Walton obviously thought that the facts of his offence were serious enough to warrant the penalty of death. The court-martial papers had then to be submitted in turn to his commanding officer, his brigade, division, corps and army commanders for their comments as to whether the sentence should be commuted or confirmed. The ultimate decision would be left to General Sir John French, the Commander-in-Chief of the BEF. On 19 March, after the court-martial documents had reached Walton's Divisional Headquarters, a senior staff officer had requested that he should be kept under medical observation "until a Medical Officer can report on the state of his mind". Although there is a brief note in Walton's court-martial file to the effect that a Medical Board was held on 20 March, there is no record of its conclusions. In spite of this, however, Sir John French found sufficient information in the papers for him to confirm the death sentence on 22 March.

After he had made his decision, the course of military justice moved swiftly to the final act. As dawn was breaking on 23 March Lance-Sergeant Walton was taken out and shot by a firing squad. He was the fourteenth British soldier to be executed for desertion since the BEF had begun their retreat from Mons at the end of the previous August.

Chapter 2

Herodotus, writing about the Greek-Persian wars, described an incident during the Battle of Marathon in 490 BC, which may well have been an example of conversion hysteria, a fairly common form of war neurosis. A large Persian army had crossed the Aegean Sea and landed in the Bay of Marathon. The Greeks, taken by surprise, had hastily assembled a numerically inferior force and charged down from the hills around the bay. After a short, ferocious engagement the invaders were defeated and driven back to their ships. In his account of the battle Herodotus wrote:

> The following prodigy occurred there: an Athenian, Epizelus, son of Cuphagoras, while fighting in the medley, and behaving valiantly, was deprived of his sight, though wounded in no part of his body, nor struck from a distance; and continued to be blind from that time for the remainder of his life.[1]

It is now recognized that a soldier's personal valour might afford him little protection against war neurosis. In the Roman army the Caesars used to select their bravest men to be Eagle-bearers in the legions. For all their courage, it was not unknown for Eagle-bearers to break down suddenly on the battlefields.[2]

Early in the seventeenth century European physicians became aware of an illness affecting soldiers on campaign, which caused them "to sink into a state of deep despair". It was especially prevalent among Spanish soldiers conscripted for service in the Netherlands during the Thirty Years War.[3] The Swiss physician Johannes Hofer published a paper in Basle about this mysterious malady in 1678. Hofer called it 'nostalgia' and likened it to "the pain which the sick person feels because he is not in his native land, or fears he is never to see it again". The ailment originated in the brain, he said, as the result of a disordered imagination. He described the symptoms of nostalgia as being "a continuing melancholy, incessant thinking of home, disturbed sleep or insomnia, weakness, loss of appetite, anxiety, cardiac palpitation, stupor and fever".[4]

Hofer considered that nostalgia was only curable if the yearning to return home could be satisfied, but that the disease could be very grave, even mortal, if circumstances made this impossible. For immediate treatment, he recommended the use of purgatives. Insomnia and restlessness could best be rectified by "the administration of narcotic mixtures".[5]

A medical directory published in 1755 described nostalgia as "a very specific disease, which was most commonly found among the Swiss, and arises chiefly from a passionate longing for their native land."[6] However, the illness was widely recognized by then as being endemic in armies generally. In 1754 the Physician-in-Ordinary to the King of France put forward a theory that "tedium and vexation" has caused nostalgia among French soldiers.[7] A few years later an Austrian physician reverted to Hofer's view. He said:

> When young men, who are still growing, are forced to enter military service and thus lose all hope of returning safe and sound to their beloved homeland, they become sad, taciturn, listless, solitary, musing, full of sighs and moans. Finally, they cease to pay attention and become indifferent to everything which the maintenance of life requires of them. This disease is called nostalgia. Neither medicaments, nor arguments, nor promises, nor threats of punishment are able to produce any improvement.[8]

Dominique Larrey, a military surgeon in Napoleon's army, regarded nostalgia as a form of insanity. He described the course of the disease in a medical essay, published in 1821.[9] Nostalgic patients suffered from fantasies, he wrote. They thought of their homes as comfortable and enchanting, no matter how mean and poverty-stricken they might be, and they visualized their relations and friends, "richly-clothed,

8

advancing towards them with affectionate greetings". Initially the patient had a feeling of oppression and weariness and he was continually stretching and sighing. Also, he became constipated and felt wandering pains in various parts of his body. Next, he developed a fever, a sense of numbness and a partial paralysis of his stomach and his diaphragm. As a result, he suffered from gastritis or from gastro-enteritis, "with a derangement of the digestive functions". In the final stage of the disease, said Larrey, the patient entered a state of debility, accompanied by increasing mental depression and constant groaning and weeping. In this phase he had a horror of food, and even of liquids, until "At last life becomes a burden; sometime the patient commits suicide, but more often the victim surrenders to death without resistance."

Not many of Larrey's medical contemporaries were prepared to accept that nostalgia was a form of madness, but they preferred to regard it as being akin to a severe type of melancholy. Nevertheless, most of them agreed with his exposition as to the progressive stages of the illness.

Another malady which seems to have been peculiar to the military was known as "soldier's heart" or "the irritable heart of soldiers". The cardinal symptoms were exhaustion and breathlessness after moderate physical exertion, an abnormally rapid pulse-rate, pains in the area of the heart and attacks of giddiness.[10] Various theories were advanced regarding the cause of this complaint, such as overstrain, deficiency of rest and nourishment, and the tightness of army equipment. However, Dr John MacCurdy, who came over to England from the United States of America in 1917 to study the problem of shell-shock, believed that it was in fact a form of anxiety neurosis, as the functions of the heart, he said, were as often influenced by anxiety conditions.[11] Hundreds of British soldiers on the Western Front during the First World War were diagnosed as suffering from "irritable heart", without the cause of the illness ever being conclusively established.[12]

In many past campaigns soldiers have been affected by battle hysteria, but their symptoms were unexplained at the time because of the limitations of medical knowledge. Sometimes they went mad; sometimes they became mute, or blind, or paralysed, or they were affected with various other ailments. These happenings were treated as being the phenomena of warfare, and if they were recorded at all

9

specious reasons were occasionally given to account for them. Dr Patton of the University Hospital of Wales has recently recounted one such instance.[13] During the Peninsular War (1808–1814) an ancestor of his was assisting some surgeons with the wounded when he suddenly went blind. It was thought that he had poisoned his eyes by rubbing them with bloody hands. Although his condition was believed to be incurable, he did eventually recover his sight. Dr Patton has suggested that his ancestor's symptom of blindness was probably "an unconscious attempt to 'shut out' the sights of mutilation" which he had witnessed at the dressing station.

It was a rarity for soldiers in past generations to suffer from the types of war neuroses which might be classified today as "battle fatigue" or "battle exhaustion", owing to the much shorter duration of the encounters between opposing armies. In his book *The Face of Battle* the military historian John Keegan mentions that Agincourt "could have been timed in hours and minutes"; Waterloo, though part of a three-day ordeal for some regiments, "was for others a one-day affair"; and Gettysburg, "bloodiest of the battles of the American Civil War, endured for three days, from mid-morning on the first to the late afternoon of the third."[14] "By the beginning of the twentieth century," Keegan observed, "battles between large armies could occupy a fortnight. By the middle of the First World War they could last several months."[15]

It seems that many of the soldiers who fought in these comparatively short engagements fortified their valour with alcohol. This applied to the French and the English armies at Agincourt. "There was drinking in the ranks on both sides during the initial period of waiting," John Keegan has written, "and it is quite probable that many soldiers in both armies went into the mêlée less than sober, if not fighting drunk."[16] Again at Waterloo, according to Keegan's researches, "many of the soldiers had drunk spirits before the battle and continued to drink while it was in progress."[17] He tells the story of the commissary of one of the English Divisions who rolled a barrel of spirits into the middle of a square during the fighting and distributed the contents to the men.[18]

Military literature abounds with references to the drinking habits of soldiers. John Ship, who enrolled in an infantry regiment in 1797, wrote in his memoirs, "I have known some men drink enormous

10

quantities of spirituous liquor when going into action, to drive away little intruding thoughts, and to create false spirits."[19]

Until 1830 every British Soldier in the field received a daily issue of between 1⅓ and 1½ gills of rum, a gill being equal to a quarter of a pint. After 1830 troops, whether they were serving at home or abroad, were given a daily money allowance for the purchase of alcohol.[20] Many of the senior officers who gave evidence before the Royal Commission on Military Punishments in 1835 spoke about the prevalence of drunkenness among the troops, especially when they were serving overseas. One colonel described it as "the besetting sin of the British soldier".[21]

Excessive drinking by British troops in battle areas continued during the Crimean War. When Lord Raglan was concentrating his army around the Bulgarian port of Varna in 1854, prior to the invasion of the Crimea, William Russell, the correspondent of *The Times*, criticized the lack of discipline among the men. "They are to be seen," he said, "lying drunk in the kennels or in the ditches by the roadside under the blazing rays of the sun, covered with swarms of flies."[22] A year later Mrs Duberly visited Sebastopol a few days after the town had been evacuated by the Russians. She recorded in her journal that the victorious British and French soldiers were now in possession and she added, "They lay about in all directions hopelessly drunk".[23]

Because of their ignorance of hysterical conditions and the crudity of diagnosis, army doctors in the past viewed with suspicion any soldier who reported sick with an unaccountable complaint. In 1836 a physician named Hector Gavin published a book *Feigned and Fictitious Diseases* to facilitate the exposure of malingerers.[24] He began by stating why his book was so necessary:

> Recruits comparatively seldom enlist in consequence of a decided preference for a military life, but commonly in conse-quence of some domestic broil, or from a boyish fancy; sometimes for want of work and its immediate consequences, great indigence, or from folly, or intemperance. Perhaps nine-tenths of the recruits regret the measure they have taken, and are willing to practise any fraud, or adopt any means which would promise to restore them to liberty and to the society of their former acquaintances. . . . The veracity of a soldier may

11

be suspected if it be discovered that he dislikes a particular duty to which he is liable, or that he is disgusted with the service.

Gavin went on to enumerate some of the subterfuges which were attempted by malingering soldiers. If they claimed to have gone blind, without any apparent cause, "there is reason to infer that their loss of vision is only pretended." Sometimes they shammed deafness and it was difficult to determine whether the condition was true or feigned, especially if they kept up the deception "with art and perseverance". Dumbness was a frequent pretence and was occasionally successful and deaf-dumbness could be "simulated for a long time without detection". As for stammering, "The simulation of this infirmity is very easy, and comes too much within the power of every man's abilities not to be very common."

In Gavin's opinion there were no limits to the ruses which soldiers would employ to evade further military service. It was simple to fake paralysis, he said, and it was very difficult for a physician to know whether or not the condition was genuine. Men would sometimes refuse to move an arm or a leg and would insist "that they have lost the power of locomotion in their limbs". They also pretended to be suffering from epilepsy, hysteria and insanity, or else from a general indisposition. Sometimes their simulation of disease was calculated to baffle the most attentive and experienced medical officers.

Almost grudgingly Gavin admits that a state of terror could cause a soldier to become genuinely ill. "Fear," he said, "seems in some instances to have a powerful and almost wonderful depressing effect; individuals are sometimes found even to sink under its influence."

Nostalgia was seldom feigned in the British Army, said Gavin. But probably its simulation would be attended with but little chance of success because "it is almost impossible to imitate the alteration and expression of countenance, the languid appearance, and sadness, so impressed on all the features which is always present in the real disease."

According to Gavin the incidence of nostalgia in the French Army was extremely high, but this might have been due, he added, to the fact that French soldiers with nostalgia were exempted from further military service.

Chapter 3

The American Civil War played an important, though indirect, part in awakening medical opinion to the complexities of war neurosis. At that time, however, attention was mainly focused on the neurological rather than the psychiatric aspect of the problem.[1]

It was inevitable that the bitter four-year internecine struggle should have given rise to many neurotic symptoms among the opposing armies because of the sanguinary nature of the fighting, the magnitude of the casualties and the increased accuracy of the new weapons employed by both sides.

At the outbreak of hostilities in the spring of 1861 the Union and the Confederate Governments had relied on voluntary enlistment, but eventually, owing to their huge losses, they had each resorted to conscription. On the Union side the age of enlistment had been lowered from 20 to 18. Dr William A. Hammond, Surgeon-General of the U.S. Army, in his annual report in June, 1862, said that some of the serving soldiers were only 16. "Youths of this age," he commented, "are not developed, and not yet fit to endure the fatigues and deprivations of military life."[2] Dr Hammond's views were supported by the Assistant Surgeon-General, De Witt C. Peters, in an article published by the *American Medical Times* in February, 1863. Peters explained the difficulties experienced by teenage recruits:

> The fresh and youthful American volunteer leaves home flushed with patriotism, and animated by new associations. If he be from the rural districts, he is to all appearance the personification of perfect health. Stimulated by bright

13

anticipations of the future, he may resist the inroads of disease, but in a few months the novelty of long marches, guard duty, exposure, and innumerable hardships, had vanished. His mind begins to despond, and the youth is now a fair victim for some other terrible scourge that is to wreck his constitution and his hopes. . . . It is by lack of discipline, confidence, and respect that many a young soldier has become discouraged, and made to feel the bitter pangs of home-sickness, which is the usual precursor of more serious ailments. That peculiar state of mind, denominated nostalgia by medical writers, is a species of melancholy, or a mild type of insanity, caused by disappointment and a continuous longing for home.[3]

Dr Peters does not seem to have considered it to be relevant that, when the symptoms of nostalgia first appeared, the young soldiers were probably completing their training and were preparing themselves for immediate duty in the firing line.

Some military writers have called the American Civil War the last of the old-fashioned wars: others have called it the first modern war, for both sides made use of aerial reconnaissance from balloons, transmission of messages by telegraph and the movement of troops by train. There had also been considerable technological advances in armaments, most of all in effectiveness of artillery fire. The shrapnel shell, invented in 1803, opened up on bursting and showered metal fragments or bullets in all directions. The precision of shelling had been greatly enhanced a few years earlier by the introduction of "rifling", the cutting of narrow grooves inside the barrels of guns to impart a spin to projectiles at the moment of discharge, thereby giving them greater stability in flight. Furthermore, the cumbersome musket had been replaced, for general use, by the long-range infantry rifle. The inventor, Richard Gatling, patented his multi-barrel machine gun in 1862, but surprisingly, neither of the opposing armies appears to have made very much use of it in the fighting.

The increased efficiency in fire-power exacted a heavy toll on the forces of both sides. The Union army suffered 634,703 casualties, out of whom 359,528 men were killed. The figures for the Confederate army are believed to be about 483,000 casualties and around 258,000 killed.

At the outbreak of hostilities the Union and the Confederate armies had planned to evacuate their wounded from the combat zones in hospital ships. Both had been forced to abandon this idea because of the number of soldiers suffering from nostalgia who crowded on board and made it impossible for the wounded and the physically sick to be given proper attention.[4] In 1888 the United States Government published a massive report on illness and treatment in the Union army during the Civil War. It defined nostalgia in simple terms:

> A temporary feeling of depression frequently pervaded our camps on account of the discomfort, hardships, and exposures, especially when these were recognized or assumed by our volunteer soldiers to be of a preventable or uncalled for nature. During its continuance, the happiness and comforts of home arose to mind, coupled with the desire to again experience them. The natural result of existing discomfort constituted the only nostalgic influence to which our troops as a rule were subject.[5]

The "home feeling", the report went on, occasionally developed "to a morbid degree", resulting in nostalgia. During the first year of the war there had been 5213 cases of this malady among the white troops in the Union army, approximately 2.34 to every 1,000 men. In the second year the figure had risen to 3.3 cases per 1,000 men. The report does not state the proportions for the third and fourth years, but even if the rate had remained constant at 3.3, the number of nostalgia patients would have been considerable, as a total of 1,556,000 soldiers fought in the Union forces during the four years of the conflict. According to the official statistics, twelve men died of the complaint in 1863.[6]

The principal cause of nostalgia, said the report, was absence from home in new and strange surroundings, particularly when these were of a depressing character. Two types of soldier were especially prone to the condition. Firstly "young men of feeble will, highly developed imaginative faculties, and strong sexual desires"; secondly, married men who were parted from their families for the first time. The usual symptoms were "disordered digestion; increased sensibility; palpitations; illusions; a succession of morbid feelings which appeared to

15

stimulate the greater part of the disease; panics; and exaggerated uneasiness of various kinds, chiefly in regard to health." An experienced military surgeon had said about his nostalgia patients that "No ordinary means could arouse them from their mental and physical inactivity – they seemed to be callous to moral sensibility."[7]

In the course of his article in the *American Medical Times*, De Witt C. Peters, the Assistant Surgeon-General to the Union Army, gave his own enumeration of the symptoms of nostalgia:

> First, great mental dejection, loss of appetite, indifference to external influences, irregular action of the bowels, and slight hectic fever. As the disease progresses it is attended by hysterical weeping, a dull pain in the head, throbbing of the temporal arteries, anxious expression on the face, watchfulness, incontinence of urine, spermatorrhoea,* increased hectic fever, and a general wasting of all the vital powers. The disease may terminate in resolution, or run into cerebral derangement, typhoid fever, or any epidemic prevailing in the immediate vicinity, and frequently with fatal results.[8]

Dr Hammond, Peters' immediate superior in the Union army, had made an intensive study of nervous and mental diseases.[9] He had little sympathy with men who contracted nostalgia and became unfit for further military duty. The best way of preventing the malady, he said, was by providing suitable occupations for the mind and the body. He thought that soldiers who were sent to hospitals near their homes were always more liable to contract nostalgia than those who went to hospitals "in the midst or in the vicinity of the Army to which they belong".[10]

During the American Civil War a large number of men were diagnosed as suffering from "soldiers' irritable heart". The military surgeons believed that this was purely a physical condition resulting from overstrain and poor feeding. The normal symptoms were said to be palpitations, lassitude, shortness of breath and chest pains. Apart from the more severe cases, patients generally recovered after a few months' rest in hospital.[11]

---

* The frequent or excessive emission of semen without an orgasm.

In the first two years of the Civil War six men out of every 1000 were discharged from the Union army with insanity. It is impossible to tell how many of them were actually suffering from war neurosis. When Medical Officers decided that a soldier had gone mad he was discharged immediately without any arrangements being made for his journey home or for his subsequent care. This alarmed the Association of Medical Superintendents of American Institutions for the Insane and, as a result of their protests, the War Department issued an order in 1863 that in future no soldiers should be discharged from the army on grounds of insanity.[12]

In spite of the War Department's order, the Managers of the Government Hospital for the Insane reported that during the year 1863–1864 there had been an increase in the number of soldiers admitted to their institution. The reason for this, they said, was that the recruits in the Union Army at that time included "a large proportion of men who are more readily affected by the exciting causes of insanity than were to be found during the first two years of the war". In their report for the year 1864–1865 the Managers stated that 83% of the male patients admitted to the hospital had been soldiers. After treatment, just over 40% of them had recovered, but a high proportion were incurably insane.[13]

Nostalgia and irritable heart could account for many of the unusual symptoms which were manifested on or near the field of battle, but the sudden onset of paralysis remained an unexplained mystery. During the American Civil War the military surgeons originated a theory that the wind of a shell, passing close to a soldier's spine, could paralyse one or more of his limbs. This process they called "windage", and Surgeon Huntington of the Union army explained how it was brought about:

> It is now conceded by modern surgeons that, without the actual contact of the projectile, injuries can occur; on the other hand, it is admitted that slight contact from the grazing or brushing of a projectile, or the rolling motion of a cannon ball over the surface of the body, may by the weight and momentum, aided by the elasticity of the skin, effect most serious results, while little or no external evidence of such contact is left.[14]

The official *Medical and Surgical History of the Civil War* seemed to accept the concept of "windage". In cases where there was no external evidence of contact, said the authors, it was suggested that an explanation of the internal injury might be found "in the sudden and violent spasm of the voluntary muscles" which was usually the involuntary result of the near passage of a large and dangerous missile. It was known, the authors went on, that muscular action could rupture internal organs and fracture bones; it was therefore "readily conceivable that the spine might have suffered an injury although there was no actual contact with the passing shell."[15] The surprisingly high total of 20.8 out of every 1000 men were discharged from the Union army during the war owing to paralysis of one or more of their limbs.[16]

Sixteen examples were given in the official medical history of men being affected by the wind of passing shells. Eleven of them were paralysed in one or both legs and one was left with paraplegia. A 24-year-old corporal had had no paralysis, but had suffered from constant headaches and eventually he had been discharged. The last three of the cases were young privates aged 20, 18 and 17 respectively. They had been on guard duty together and were all afflicted with "windage". In hospital "they took no notice of things around them, seeming to be in deep sleep." The two older youths recovered and were returned to their unit, but the 17-year-old had died without improving.[17]

After the end of the American Civil War medical opinion remained divided as to whether or not troops could suffer traumatic effects from the wind of a passing projectile. Many surgeons and physicians were unable to accept the feasibility of "windage", though some believed that injuries could be caused by the "grazing or brushing" of a shell, even though there was no external evidence of any contact.

At the beginning of 1865 Dr George Burr, the Professor of Anatomy in the Geneva College and a former army surgeon, wrote an article in the *New York Medical Journal* contending that "serious injury to the nervous system may be met with, without the body receiving either wound or contusion". As a result the patient might suffer from partial or complete paralysis, deafness, blindness, loss of voice, rupture of the superficial blood-vessels or mental prostration.[18]

18

Dr Burr went on to say that most of his medical colleagues during the Civil War had refused to believe that injuries could be caused to a soldier simply by a shell bursting in his vicinity. However, 130 cases in military hospitals had been recorded as "compression of the brain caused by shell explosions". Out of these, seventy-one men had been returned to duty and others had been discharged because of deafness, blindness, paralysis, insanity, meningitis, spinal affections and nervous prostration. From his own experience as a military surgeon, Dr Burr was able to give several examples of the physical effects of shell-blast. A captain who had been stunned by a shell exploding near him was paralysed in one side of his body and had difficulty in speaking. Fortunately he had recovered a few months later. A regimental adjutant had also been close to a bursting shell. He had ridden to a field hospital and, when he reached it, he had been unable to dismount from his horse without assistance. "He appeared stunned, bewildered, unsteady in his movements and half-conscious of his whereabouts." For some reason he had not been detained at the hospital, but was helped on to his horse and allowed to ride away. After that he had disappeared for a while and was next heard of at his home. The adjutant had been dismissed from the service for going absent without leave. Dr Burr mentioned another case in which a shell had exploded between five and ten feet above an officer's head and had left him paralysed, deaf and only able to speak with difficulty.

In a book published in New York just after the First World War Dr Frederick Peterson analysed the official figures for diseases and illnesses in the Union army during the Civil War. He came to the conclusion that the majority of the nostalgia cases, and some of the men described as having sunstroke, were in reality suffering from war neurosis. He also thought that a number of soldiers with symptoms of war neurosis were incorrectly diagnosed as having epilepsy or malaria.[19]

The eminent Philadelphia neurologist Silas Weir Mitchell, who had served as a surgeon in the Union Army, referred to the subject of malingering in an article he wrote with another neurologist as the conclusion of the Civil War. The principal offenders, they said, were not the soldiers who "feigned epilepsies, paralyses and the like", but those with real diseases who pretended to be a lot worse than they

19

really were, or else made out that they were still sick when they had fully recovered.[20]

One form of malingering in the Union army which had virtually ceased in 1863 was shammed insanity. After the War Department's edict forbidding the discharge of insane soldiers, even service in the front line must have seemed preferable to indefinite detention in a military institution for lunatics.[21]

Chapter 4

In 1904 Dr Paul Jacoby, the Physician-in-Chief of a Provincial Asylum in Russia, drew attention to the large number of soldiers who had become insane during the Franco-Prussian War of 1870–71 and the Russo-Turkish war of 1877–1878.[1] Insanity had also been common in the Russian army fighting against China in 1900, when many of the men who went mad were shot by their comrades to save them from being captured and tortured by the Chinese. Dr Jacoby attributed the high incidence of derangement to the fact that the privations and fatigues of active service, the nervous tension caused by ever-present danger, the frequent mental shocks, alcoholism and wounds all predisposed to madness.

Dr Thomas W. Salmon, who had made a study of "shell-shock" in the First World War, was of the opinion that the high rate of insanity during previous wars "was due, in part at least, to the failure to recognize the true nature of severe neurosis".[2]

Until midway through the nineteenth century, soldiers with war neurosis would have had little chance of recovering in a civilian lunatic asylum. These institutions were not infirmaries for treating the sick: they were more like penitentiaries for the incarceration of sub-humans, where inmates were kept in chains and were subjected to the cruellest punishments. During the Middle Ages it was believed in Europe that the insane were possessed by devils. As a consequence, they were regarded with fear and loathing. During the seventeenth century the idea of demonic possession was replaced by the view that madness was caused by witchcraft and the insane continued to be flogged and tortured. In British colonial America they were sometimes put up for auction and their new masters were left with the choice between exploiting them or treating them with humanity.

In 1792 Philippe Pinel, the French medical reformer, horrified his fellow physicians by "striking the chains" from the lunatics at Bicetre and Salpêtrière, two of the largest asylums in France, and by calling on the world to realize the barbaric way in which the insane were being oppressed. His plea had little effect and, twenty years later, Jean Esquirol, another French physician, asserted that everywhere in Europe lunatics were treated worse than criminals and were being reduced to the level of animals. He had seen them, he said, in their narrow filthy cells, naked and covered in rags, and with only straw to protect them against the cold. They were kept without air or light, fastened with chains in dens not fit for wild beasts.

Gradually, during the early part of the nineteenth century, lunatic asylums were being turned into hospitals, but the transformation was slow. A House of Commons committee in 1815 condemned the inhuman conditions existing at Bedlam, the notorious London madhouse. In the 1840s Dorothea Dix, a teacher from Maine, exposed the fact that lunatics and criminals were being imprisoned together in some certain American jails. And as recently as 1841 some asylums in Belgium still kept their inmates in fetters.

The large number of men diagnosed as suffering from "irritable heart" during the American Civil War continued to mystify medical opinion long after the conflict was over. Dr Henry Harthorne, in a paper he contributed to the *American Journal of Medical Science* in 1864, described the most familiar symptoms of the complaint as being rapidity of the pulse, acceleration of the heart's movements on the slightest exertion, shortness of breath and weakness of the cardiac muscles.[3] In 1871 the same journal published an article by Dr Da Costa, who had treated about 300 soldiers with "irritable hearts" at a hospital in Philadelphia during the Civil War. He gave the case-history of one of his patients[4]:

A man, three months or so on active service, was seized with diarrhoea, annoying yet not severe, soon rejoined, and then noticed that he could not bear exertion as well as formerly, out-of-breath and unable to keep up with his comrades; dizziness and palpitation; accoutrements oppressed him, yet

22

otherwise he seemed well and healthy. Sought advice; was sent to hospital where his persistent quick heart confirmed his story.

Dr Da Costa mentioned that some of his patients had digestive disturbances and some had intermittent attacks of fever during which their pulse rate dropped and became erratic. After the other symptoms had passed, he said, "the irritable condition of the heart remained, and only very slowly did it get normal, or it failed to do so at all".[5]

The British Government was so concerned about the prevalence of "the irritable heart of soldiers" that in 1864 it appointed a committee, consisting of three generals and two doctors, to enquire into heart disorders in the army. During the next four years the Committee issued a series of reports, in one of which they said that the condition described as "irritable heart" was due to "an extreme excitability of the heart, combined with some, but not great, enlargement. During rest, this kind of heart beats easily, but on the least exertion its action becomes irregular and the man becomes breathless." Eventually the committee recommended a modification in the standard pattern of equipment used by the British army because, in their opinion, it tended to restrict the free movement of a soldier's heart. Their recommendation was adopted, but it brought about no reduction in the number of men reporting sick with this complaint.[6]

A few years later a small group of senior Medical Officers in the United States forces came up with the theory that "irritable heart" resulted from 'setting-up drill'; the type of physical training used by the army. They said that it caused an over-expansion of the chest and the consequent enlargement of the heart gave rise to cardiac irritability. Their suggestion was taken so seriously by the military authorities that setting-up drill was discontinued. However, there were no beneficial results, so the cause of the "illness" continued to be a medical mystery.[7]

A new dimension to the study of soldiers' ailments was added by the American neurologist Silas Weir Mitchell. During the Civil War Dr Mitchell had been on the staff of a hospital in Philadelphia, where he had taken a particular interest in patients who were suffering from shock, occasioned by gunshot wounds to various parts of their bodies. He was, in fact, observing the symptoms of post-traumatic neurosis, but he ascribed them to damage sustained by the nerve centres. In a book on nerve injuries, published in 1872, he wrote:

> One of the gravest of the instant consequences of nerve injuries is that which is known as "shock". This is commonly described as a condition in which the patient becomes cold, faint, and trembling; the pulse is small and fluttering; there is a great mental depression and disquietude; incoherence of speech and thought; the surface becomes covered by a cold sweat; there is nausea, perhaps vomiting, and relaxation of the sphincters. . . . This state of shock, so well known to the surgeon, is simply a reflex effect of the injuries of nerves, large or small. In general, it affects in varying proportion the great nerve centres which preside over circulation, respiration, and voluntary movement.[8]

He could find no explanation, he said, for the fact that sometimes the brain was affected, sometimes the heart, and sometimes the motor centre for the leg or the arm. After a bullet had crushed a nerve, a "tremendous shock" was transmitted to the spine and was immediately re-directed to one of the nerve centres.

Dr Mitchell gave several examples of the cases he had come across at the hospital. A colonel, who had been wounded in the wrist, had run along the line of his regiment in a half-crazed state of excitement and then had fallen to the ground insensible. Another officer, formerly noted for his bravery, was wounded in the heel and had instantly started to behave like an insane person, in "a condition of the utmost trepidation". One of Dr Mitchell's patients was paralysed in all four limbs, yet he had only sustained a flesh wound in the thigh. A man with a similar wound had been partially paralysed in his right leg and arm.

During the eighteenth century there had been a growing interest in the nervous system, and William Cullen, an Edinburgh physician, had coined the term "neurosis" to cover all nervous disorders.[9] The nervous problems resulting from prolonged periods of mental stress had received particular attention in the nineteenth century. The distinguished American neurologist George Beard treated many patients suffering from "nervous exhaustion", which he believed to be a

24

common illness in the United States. In 1880 he published his book, *A Practical Treatise on Nervous Exhaustion (Neurasthenia)*, which was still regarded as a leading work on the subject long after his death.[10] Neurasthenia became a fashionable illness in Victorian society and the term was used to describe every form of nervous ailment.[11] However, the existence of the condition was not universally accepted. Dr Thomas Glynn, the Professor of Medicine at the University of Liverpool, wrote in 1910:

> When I was a student, neurasthenia was not recognized, and hospital patients who exhibited no signs of organic disease, or some familiar nervous disorder, were usually set down as malingerers. With increased knowledge, we now take a more humane and rational view of these cases, but as our diagnosis of pure neurasthenia largely depends on the statements of the subject under investigation, and not on objective signs, we have to guard against deception.[12]

The belief that soldiers could sustain mental and physical injuries without receiving any visible wounds was extended by Sir John Erichsen when he applied a similar proposition to civilians who suffered shock as the result of an accident. Erichsen, a distinguished London surgeon, originated the diagnosis of "railway spine" to cover most of the emotional symptoms exhibited by his patients who had been involved in railway accidents.

Railway travel had begun in England in 1830 with the opening of the Liverpool and Manchester line, for both passengers and freight. Soon "railway mania" was obsessing the public imagination and hundreds of miles of new railtrack were being laid every year. By 1870 it was estimated that there were 13,500 miles of railroad, spread out all over parts of the country. The steam locomotive became the principal form of long-distance and even short-distance travel, both for its convenience and its rapidity. In those early days accidents were frequent, caused mainly by collisions and derailments. An additional hazard was created by trains travelling at speeds beyond the capabilities of the system. At the start they carried their passengers at about 35 miles an hour: by the close of the century they were travelling at 50 miles an hour or more.

25

Sir John Erichsen explained the nature of "railway spine" at a lecture he gave in 1866 to the students of the University College Hospital, where he was professor of surgery. He told them:

> Concussions of the spine and the spinal cord not infrequently occur in the ordinary accidents of civil life, but none more frequently or with greater severity than those which are sustained by passengers who have been subjected to the violent shock of a railway collision. . . . In no ordinary accident can the shock be so great as those which occur on the railways. The rapidity of the movement, the momentum of the person injured, the suddenness of its arrest, the helplessness of the sufferer, and the natural perturbation of mind that must disturb the bravest, all the circumstances that of necessity increase the severity of the resulting injury to the nervous system, and justly cause these cases to be considered as some-what exceptional from ordinary accidents. This had led some surgeons to designate that particular affection of the spine, met with in these cases, as the "railway spine".[13]

The cause of this condition, said Erichsen, was the shaking or jarring of the spinal cord. At the time of the accident the victim was usually unaware he had been severely injured. He might feel a bit giddy and confused, but he imagined himself to be completely unscathed, or, at the most, to have suffered some superficial cuts or bruises. Erichsen went on:

> When he reaches home, the effects of the injury he has sustained begin to manifest themselves. A revulsion of feeling takes place. He bursts into tears, becomes unusually talkative, and is excited. He cannot sleep, or, if he does, he wakes suddenly with a feeling of alarm. . . . After a time, which varies much in different cases, from a day or two to a week or more, he finds that he is unfit for exertion and unable to attend to business.

In a short while, Erichsen told his students, the condition of the patient deteriorates even more. He loses his bodily energy and his mental

26

capacity. His memory becomes defective and his thoughts confused. He usually has trouble with his vision, and sometimes with his hearing or his ability to taste or to smell. Even worse, the "nervous power" of his limbs could be affected. It might be one limb, it might be more. Indeed, he could lose the complete use of an arm and both his legs.

It is rather surprising that medical attention never seems to have been drawn to the similarity between many of the symptoms attributed to "railway spine" and those which were believed to result from "windage" or from gunshot wounds to the nerve centres of the body. Perhaps it was thought that soldiers could never suffer from the sense of "helplessness" and the "perturbation of mind" which Erichsen had described in his exposition on the new disorder.

In actions for personal damages against the railway companies during the latter part of the nineteenth century it was customary for plaintiffs to claim that they were suffering from "railway spine" resulting from accidents. There were plenty of doctors willing to support them with medical evidence and they were usually successful. It was alleged by cynics that many of them recovered remarkably quickly from their impairments directly the legal proceedings were over.[14]

Erichsen's theory encountered strong criticism by several highly-respected authorities. Herbert Page, consultant-surgeon to the London and North-Western Railway, citing 250 recent patients of his own, stated categorically that the spinal cord was very seldom injured in these accidents. He contended that the great majority of the victims were, in reality, suffering from the after-affects of nervous shock.[15] James Putnam, a leading American neurologist, agreed. "In spite of all the attention which has been given to the subject," he said, "we know of no pathological state of the spinal cord to which the name of concussion could properly be applied, and it is evident that some at least of the symptoms usually designated by it can be grouped under other headings."[16] Erichsen's theory was also criticized by the French physician Jean-Martin Charcot, a specialist in nervous diseases, who believed that the so-called "railway spine" cases were often suffering from nothing more than hysteria.[17]

Looking back on this controversy in 1910, Professor Glynn reached a conclusion which was indirectly relevant to some forms of soldiers' neuroses. He wrote:

27

Emotional disturbance probably plays a more important part in the production of the traumatic neurosis than physical injury. A depressing emotion, such as terror, may in itself give rise to a hysteria or neurasthenia, and instances are not infrequently met with where these disorders have been excited by accidents, which, though trivial, have occasioned much apprehension.[18]

Chapter 5

During the nineteenth century there was an increasing awareness of the fundamental importance of the subconscious mind in the control of human behaviour. This helped to reveal the true nature of war neurosis.

Although Franz Anton Mesmer was not directly concerned with the inter-relationship of the conscious and the unconscious elements in the mind, he prepared the groundwork for the psychiatrists and psycho-analysts of later years. Mesmer, who was born in 1734, practised as a physician in Vienna. He became interested in the theory that astrological healing influences could be transmitted to the bodies of sick persons through invisible fluids by stroking their skins with a magnet.[1] When he was in his early forties he formed the belief that, if he were to dispense with magnets, he would be able to convey these curative fluids to his patients himself by the employment of a myste-rious occult power. From then on he used to arrange therapeutic sessions in an atmosphere resembling a seance more than a medical consultation. The patients would sit round a large vat, in a darkened room, holding hands. He would subject them to a trance-like condition by a process which became known as "mesmerism" and would pass among them, touching them with a hand or with a rod. Despite the fact that he brought about some spectacular cures, Mesmer was accused of witchcraft by his fellow Viennese physicians and eventually he was forced to abandon his practice and leave Austria.[2]

In 1778 Mesmer settled in Paris where he carried on with the same methods which he had used in Vienna. The Parisians were enormously impressed with his numerous successful treatments and he very soon built up a lucrative practice. The theatricality of Mesmer's consultations increased. He started to dress as a magician. He hung his dimly-lit consulting room with mirrors and soft music was played to his patients during the sessions. When Mesmer had been in Paris for six years King Louis XVI set up a committee of scientists and physicians to investigate his techniques. Their report was extremely sceptical. There were no invisible magnetic fluids, they said, and his cures were solely due to the imagination of his patients. The result of this authoritative appraisal was that mesmerism was discredited and was associated with charlatanism and chicanery. Mesmer himself remained in Paris until the outbreak of the French Revolution when he emigrated to London.

Mesmerism continued to be officially accepted in Germany, Prussia and Denmark as a genuine form of medical treatment, but it was totally rejected in other parts of Europe, where its curative effect ceased to be attributed to any external source and came to be recognized as emanating from his patients' own minds.[3]

The leading members of the British medical profession treated mesmerism with suspicion and mistrust. In 1838 Dr John Elliotson was forced to resign his position as a senior physician on the staff of University College Hospital because it was known that he was practising the system. One of Elliotson's contemporaries, James Esdaile, who worked as a government surgeon in Calcutta, made extensive use of the mesmeric trance in carrying out major operations, even the amputation of limbs. Although admitting that Esdaile could counteract pain, the medical authorities frowned upon his methods, and he, too, was dismissed. In fact it was not until the late 1840s that a patient who was about to undergo surgery could be given a general anaesthetic.

James Braid, a Manchester surgeon, first attempted to make the concept of the mesmeric trance acceptable to British medicine, under the name of "hypnotism". In 1841 he became keenly interested in mesmerism as a way of inducing sleep, for he saw its therapeutic possibilities in the treatment of nervous ailments, as well as its usefulness in surgery. He invented the name "hypnosis", derived from the Greek word for sleep, for the procurement of the trance-like condition and he discovered that it could be brought about by his patients concentrating their gaze upon bright, inanimate objects. Braid practised hypnotism regularly and successfully, but it did not find favour with medical opinion at the time because it continued to be associated with Mesmer and, accordingly, bore the taint of charlatanism.

One person who was greatly impressed with Braid's researches was the celebrated French neurologist Jean-Martin Charcot, who has been called the founder of modern neurology. One of his greatest services to medicine was the persuasion of the medical profession that hysteria was a serious disease and that men as well as women could be affected with it.[4] Charcot decided to make use of hypnotism to try to discover if there was any organic basis for hysteria.

Another French physician to perform a valuable service to medicine, and in particular to the understanding of neurology, was Pierre Janet. In 1889, at the invitation of Charcot, he became Director of the Psychology Laboratory at the medical school of Salpêtrière, at that time the largest mental institution in Paris. Janet was a keen exponent of hypnotism, both for his treatments and his researches. While he was at Salpêtrière he investigated many different hysterical conditions, and one of his conclusions was that hysteria could cause amnesia, paralysis, loss of speech, stammering, blindness, and deafness. Janet and Charcot both felt that psychology and medicine were complementary and should be pursued together. This view was shared by Dr Morton Prince, a Boston physician and psychologist who taught neurology in the Harvard Medical School during the 1890s.

Physicians from all over the world used to come to Paris in order to study neurology under Jean-Martin Charcot. One of his pupils, in 1885, was Sigmund Freud, then aged 29 and working at a hospital in Vienna. Freud had visited France five years previously and had become very interested in the use of hypnosis as a method of investigating the contents of a person's mind. He thought it might be helpful in the treatment of most neurotic disorders. However, when he returned to Vienna he found that he was unable to bring the majority of his patients into a hypnotic state and that, even when he could do so, the cures he managed to achieve were by no means permanent. So he decided to abandon hypnotism in favour of "free association".

The devising of "free association" as a means of investigating the deep-rooted, subconscious motivation of neurosis is considered to be one of Freud's great contributions to psychotherapy.[5] His patients would recline on a couch, completely relaxed, and would be encouraged to disclose the thoughts that came into their minds, however improbable, repugnant or irrelevant. Freud found this to be an effective way of restoring their forgotten memories, and thereby revealing the sources of their hysteric anxieties.

Freud was also the founder of psychoanalysis, a therapeutic method of treating neurotic disorders, which he described for the first time in a paper he published in 1896.[6] He used to find that, although his patients were able to recollect some of the circumstances surrounding the origins of their neurosis, there were other relevant incidents which had been repressed into their subconscious minds. "The doctrine of repression," he said, "is the foundation stone on which the whole structure of psychoanalysis rests."[7] It was the purpose of the psychoanalyst to relocate his patients' hidden memories in the accessible precincts of their conscious thoughts.

Wishes and impulses were repressed, according to Freud, because they were completely contrary to a person's normal character. The repression gave rise to a mental conflict which frequently resulted in the emergence of some neurotic symptom. For instance, a dutiful soldier who was overcome with fear before going into action, and was extremely ashamed of his weakness, might develop a hysterical paralysis of a leg or an arm. This disability would prevent him from fighting, so he would achieve his desire to avoid the battle; at the same time he would retain his self-esteem as he has not behaved with cowardice or dishonour.[8]

During the twentieth century recurrent nightmares were to become a well-recognized symptom of war neurosis. Freud was the first psychiatrist to place the interpretation of dreams on a scientific basis, because they were, he said, "the language of the unconscious". He always attached great importance to the contents of his patients' dreams in helping him to discover the causes of their neuroses.[9]

The Swiss psychiatrist Carl Jung worked closely with Freud and confirmed many of his theories, but he could not agree with Freud's insistence on the sexual origin of neuroses. Another psychiatrist with an international reputation, the Austrian Alfred Adler, agreed with many of Freud's beliefs, but also disputed his view that mental illness was traceable to sexual conflicts in early childhood.

For the most part medical opinion in England was opposed to the practice of psychoanalysis and to the notions of Freud and other continental theorists. It was thought that exploration of the mind, and the search for subconscious motivation, might undermine a patient's mental stability. Above all, in the eyes of the majority of English physicians, the new teaching of this small band of psychiatrists, apart from being utterly ill-founded, was a challenge to traditional values and to medical orthodoxies.[10]

Chapter 6

In 1900 Professor Richet of the Physiology Department in the Faculty of Medicine in Paris estimated that about 14,000,000 men had died in battle during the nineteenth century. This total, he said, included 8,000,000 killed in the Napoleonic Wars, 800,000 in the Franco-Prussian War, 500,000 in the American Civil War, and 300,000 in the Crimean War. An Editorial in the *British Medical Journal*, after repeating Professor Richet's figures, commented:

> If to these who died in the "stricken field" we add the number of broken, disabled soldiers, the widows and the children who suffered, we have indeed a huge budget of slaughter, a record of Christian activity, that almost makes one despair.[1]

One category of "broken" soldiers who particularly concerned Dr Paul Jacoby, Physician in Chief of the Orel Asylum in Russia, was those who had become insane on the battlefield. Even as far back as 1904 he was voicing a fear that the recent advances of weapon technology had added greatly to the nervous strain of the combatants and it was likely that the new forms of shock would produce new forms of neurosis and mental disturbance. He strongly advocated that on future campaigns every army should have special psychiatric units to attend to neurotic casualties, as medical officers already had more than enough to do in looking after the physically sick and the wounded. There were grave objections, said Dr Jacoby, to putting insane patients among the ordinary occupants in military hospitals, and if they were treated immediately in separate tents they would stand a far better chance of recovery.[2]

Britain had become involved in another war in 1899, this time against the Boers in South Africa. The reasons for the dispute were wholly insufficient to justify the waste of life and the huge financial cost of the two-and-a-half-year struggle which lay ahead. Paul Kruger, the President of the Transvaal, had refused the British Government's request that he should grant civic rights to the numerous immigrants, mostly from Britain, who were settling in his country to work in the newly-discovered gold fields of the Rand. For his part, Kruger was deeply distrustful of the British Government's attitude towards the Transvaal and of their plans to reinforce the British garrison in South Africa.

Before the fighting began, the Orange Free State joined with the Boers, enabling them to raise an army of about 50,000 well-equipped mounted infantry, plentifully supported by modern artillery pieces which had been purchased in Germany. At that time the entire British garrison in South Africa consisted of 14,700 regular soldiers. In addition, 10,000 troops were on their way from India.

In the early stages of the war the Boers had all the military successes. Apart from the fact that they had the best mounted infantry in the world, with every soldier a skilled rider and a marksman, the out-numbered British were fighting in a hostile country, an unknown terrain, and with vast lines of communication. At home in Britain the news of the initial defeats was received in a mood of shocked humili-ation, which gave way to an upsurge of anger and of patriotic fervour. A statute was rushed through Parliament making it possible for the part-time soldiers of the Militia to serve overseas and Queen Victoria issued a personal appeal to all retired officers and other ranks of the regular army to re-enlist for a short-term engagement. There was no scarcity of volunteers, and no lack of new temporary units formed specifically for service against the Boers. In an atmosphere of vacuous jingoism, the cheering crowds and the military bands lined the quay-sides whenever the troopships were setting sail for South Africa.

Meanwhile the unrelenting battle continued. An Irish Colonel, whose battalion was pinned down by Boer fire and were unable to bury their dead, wrote in his diary:

Oh those dead! How still and uncouth they lay, all dreadful
and discoloured by three days of tropical sun, and three damp

oppressive nights. Who can say there is any beauty in death? Certainly there is none in violent death.[3]

A group of doctors working at a military hospital in South Africa wrote an account of the various types of wounds and illnesses with which they had been dealing.[4] The conditions of active service, they said, were eminently favourable to the development of all sorts of functional disorders* in the nervous system. This provided malingerers with ample opportunities for deception and Medical Officers always treated such cases with suspicion. Genuine functional disorders, like paralysed limbs, could occur among wounded patients, or among others of an intensely neurotic, emotional, or even a hysterical disposition, "whose nervous systems were highly strung by the strain of campaigning, the anxiety of outpost duties, and the want of proper sleep, often for many nights in succession". They gave several examples. A Private in a Scottish Regiment had had his helmet lifted off his head by an exploded shell. "He was not wounded or hurt, but he lay on the ground for two hours unable to rise." When he was taken back to a base hospital he was found to be very feeble, bodily and mentally, and he had a constant headache. Another case of a functional disorder was a patient – they did not give his rank – near whom a shell had exploded without causing him any evident injury. "He became deaf and dumb forthwith. He remained for weeks in this condition, but we are told that when on board ship on the way to England he woke up one morning to find he had completely recovered both speech and hearing."

The doctors went on to express the opinion that officers were more likely than other ranks to suffer from functional disorders. The majority of private soldiers, they said, were "of stolid disposition". They had an utter absence of imagination, no curiosity about the future and no recollection of "the past stirring events in which they had taken part". On the other hand, many officers who had been in battle were troubled by "a tendency to emotional outbursts, which have sometimes taken the form of irresistible fits of weeping on the slightest excitement".

The book contained a very brief section on Mental Disorders, in which it was stated:

* A functional disorder is a mental disorder without any discernible cause.

36

The boundary line between neurasthenia and certifiable mental unsoundness is often ill-defined and easily over-stepped. It is not surprising, therefore, that a number of cases of mental unsoundness should occur. In fact, considering the extremely harassing nature of the military operations, it is rather remarkable that we did not see more of such cases . . . We have heard, however, of at least three officers who committed suicide.

In his authoritative study of the care and treatment of mental diseases in the British Army, Dr Thomas W. Salmon has suggested that the high insanity rate during the Boer War was due, in part at least, to a failure to recognize the true nature of severe neuroses, similar to those grouped under the term "Shell-Shock" in the First World War.[5] Some idea of the general attitude to war neurosis at that time can be gathered from a passage in the memoirs of George Lynch, a War Correspondent with the British forces, who was returning home from South Africa in the same ship as a number of sick and wounded men. He said that nine soldiers on board were suffering from complete mental breakdowns as a result of their experiences in battle. "Their brains," he explained, "had been incapable of withstanding the strain upon their nerves and they had gone mad."[6]

In October, 1901, Charles Morris, a London surgeon, described the wounds and illnesses of some of the casualties from South Africa who had been admitted to his hospital. Among the soldiers were a number suffering from nervous shock, and he said about them:

A most remarkable evidence of the privation, exhaustion, and mental strain that many had to pass through was seen in the cases of neurasthenia that occurred. It was terrible to see the condition of fine strapping men, produced in this way, which led them to shrink from the slightest touch and to shed tears like children.[7]

In March, 1902, the Boers, after a series of defeats, sued for peace. By then the British Army in South Africa numbered more than 440,000 men. About 45,000 British soldiers had been killed or wounded, or had died of disease.

Almost exactly two years later war broke out in the Far East between Japan and Russia, after Japanese forces made a surprise attack on Russian warships lying at anchor in the naval base at Port Arthur. A German doctor, working in Japan at the time, has described the symptoms of a captured Russian naval lieutenant whom he treated for "neurasthenia" at his hospital. Presumably in the initial action two Japanese sailors had boarded the Lieutenant's ship and tried to strangle him. He had succeeded in escaping by jumping overboard, dragging his assailants with him. In the sea he became unconscious and he only came to again when he was in bed at the hospital. During his convalescence he had suffered from fainting fits, breathlessness and hystero-epileptic convulsions, although he had sustained no apparent physical injury. At one point his breathing had became so laboured it was feared that he might die of suffocation and the German doctor decided he would have to have a tracheotomy. After that, his symptoms, apart from occasional bouts of breathlessness, had disappeared.[8]

The Russo-Japanese War was notable for the fact that the Russian Army broke new ground by establishing a separate forward clearing hospital where psychiatric casualties could be cared for by specialist doctors. This military innovation was extensively reported in French and German medical journals at the time and it was fully described in an American journal five years after the war ended. It was ignored by the British medical papers, although observers from Britain had been attached to both the opposing armies, and it was not mentioned at all in the War Office review of the treatment of the sick and wounded in the Russo-Japanese War which was published in 1908.[9]

Captain R.L. Richards of the United States Medical Corps, one of the American observers during the war, wrote a comprehensive account in 1910 of the treatment of "mental and nervous diseases" in the Russian Army.[10] The total number of soldiers in this category was unusually high, he said, reaching about 1,500 in 1904 and about 2,000 during the subsequent year. They were sent back from the firing line to a small psychiatric hospital at Harbin in Manchuria, which served as a forward collecting centre, and they remained there under observation by a psychiatrist until they were well enough to return to Russia.

It is interesting to note that Captain Richards refers to all the patients suffering from mental and nervous disorders as being "insane". The average time spent by each patient at Harbin, he says, was 15 to 16 days. They were then taken by train to Moscow, some 5,300 miles away, a journey which should have taken about eighteen days, but which had often lasted as long as thirty days if the trains were delayed. The other ranks travelled in special compartments with barred windows. The surgeon and the nursing sisters who were accompanying their party shared a second-class compartment with the officer-patients. Later in the war the other ranks were put into eight specially-prepared coaches equipped with heavy glass windows and separate isolation cells. In cold weather the compartments were heated with stoves. Towards the end of the journey, says Richards, "the patients were always irritable, adapted themselves to the circumstances of the train less readily, and their hallucinations became more acute."

The number of "insane" military patients was increasing every month and a point was reached when they exceeded the resources of the Army Medical Department. It was therefore arranged that the Red Cross Society of Russia would start to look after them. Harbin was becoming so overcrowded that several other psychiatric hospitals had to be opened in forward areas. Eventually, by January, 1905, soldiers suffering from mental and nervous illnesses were distributed among all the regular military hospitals.

When the patients from Harbin and the other forward psychiatric centres reached Moscow they were detained in hospitals under further observation. There had been complaints that they were sometimes discharged before they had fully recovered, and that others were returned to the front line only to break down again.

The patients who had to undergo the discomfort of the long and wearying train journey from Harbin to Moscow were fortunate compared with the soldiers who were diagnosed as suffering from mental diseases while serving with the garrison at Port Arthur. These men were sent back to Russia by sea and they were confined in the hold of a ship for the duration of the six-week voyage. On one occasion, according to Dr Jacoby, the Japanese had captured a transport vessel returning to Russia with "fourteen insane soldiers" on board.[11]

Although the Russo-Japanese War aroused a certain amount of medical interest and speculation concerning the mental and nervous disorders of the battlefield, the true nature of war neurosis was still enshrouded in ignorance and confusion. Captain Richards believed that a soldier's experiences in action sometimes caused him to develop epilepsy. "The terrors of war and the exhaustion following prolonged exertion," he said, "brought to light epileptic conditions in people not previously suspected of such a condition."[12] A German neurologist expressed the view in 1906 that troops in battle could suffer from a severe mental derangement which did not affect them in times of peace. "The patient lies for weeks," he went on, "without any movement, staring at the wall. He usually eats if food is placed in his mouth. He has hallucinations, but they do not influence him in his movements."[13] A different conclusion was reached by a doctor from Wiesbaden who told a European medical congress that the nervous troubles he had observed among wounded Russian officers in the recent war had been similar to those which were manifested by civilians affected by traumatic neurosis or "railway brain".[14] This opinion was shared by a leading German neurologist. In a paper published in 1906 he stated that the shock of battle was not, by itself, sufficient to cause serious mental disorders. The most immediate results it could engender were hysterical excitement and confusion. "These usually clear up within a few days," he said, "but irritability, fearfulness and emotional instability remain for weeks."[15]

In the course of his account of the treatment of mental disorders in the Russo-Japanese War, Captain R.L. Richards made the prescient comment:

> A future war will call at least equally large numbers of men into action. The tremendous endurance, bodily and mental, required for the days of fighting over increasingly large areas, and the mysterious and widely destructive effects of modern artillery fire will test men as they have never been tested before. We can surely count then on a much larger percentage of mental diseases requiring our attention in a future war.[16]

This controversy was almost unnoticed in Britain. Perhaps it seemed irrelevant. G.M. Trevelyan has said that no great country except English-speaking America had ever been so utterly civilian in thought and practice as Victorian England. Due to a century's immunity from great wars and from any serious national danger, "Englishmen thought of the problems of life in terms of peace and security."[17] Their small professional army, consisting of highly-trained soldiers led by ex-public school officers, was quite sufficient in peacetime for distant colonial expeditions and campaigns. It was expected, if necessary, to fight to the last man and the last round. Henry Newbold epitomized the national concept of the British soldier's devotion to duty in the second stanza of his poem Vitai Lampada, which was first published in 1898:

> The sand of the desert is sodden red, –
> Red with the wreck of a square that broke:–
> The Gatling's jammed and the Colonel dead,
> And the regiment blind with dust and smoke.
> The river of death has brimmed its banks,
> And England's far, and honour a name,
> But the voice of a schoolboy rallies the ranks:
> "Play up! play up! and play the game!"[18]

Chapter 7

At the beginning of the First World War in August, 1914, the French, the German and the British Governments all believed that their struggle would be over in a few months. All three nations were confident that their armies would achieve complete victory in that time.

Britain had not considered herself to be a great military power, although she thought her Navy second to none. In October, 1913, the total strength of the British Army, with worldwide commitments, had been 247,250, supported by reserves of 61,048 officers and men. The Territorial Army, which had been formed in 1908, numbered 276,618, and was a force of barely-trained, part-time soldiers, ineligible for service overseas. Only six regular army divisions, consisting of about 160,000 troops, were available for the British Expeditionary Force which was sent to France between 12 and 17 August, 1914.[1]

Lord Kitchener, the newly-appointed British Secretary for War, did not share the general optimism about the probable duration of the conflict. He surprised his colleagues at the first cabinet meeting he attended by forecasting that the war would continue for three years and that Britain would require to raise an army of several million men. He said that he wanted the first 100,000 recruits immediately, to be trained for action with the BEF. The Prime Minister, Herbert Asquith, considered that any form of compulsory military service would be politically unpopular and that the necessary reinforcements would have to be provided by voluntary enlistment.[2]

Kitchener then launched a massive recruitment campaign which was immediately successful. In a single week at the beginning of September 175,000 men volunteered for service with the Army, and by the end of the month the total intake numbered around 750,000. Over the next few months the figure rose to almost a million, and in addition more than 60% of the Territorial Army had declared their willingness to serve overseas.[3] The recruits, mostly young men in the prime of life, were fired by patriotism and a romantic sense of adventure; they had no conception of the reality of warfare. Because Britain was still riddled with consciousness of class the new officers had to be 'gentlemen', which meant that they must have been educated at public schools, or perhaps at one of the superior grammar schools. RC Sherriff the author of the moving play *Journey's End*, based upon his own experiences on the Western Front, was refused a commission during the first month of the war. He was told by the officer who interviewed him, "Our instructions are that all applicants for commissions must be selected from recognized public schools and yours is not among them."[4] But the time was fast approaching when the British would not be able to be so discriminatory.

The First Battle of Ypres began on 10 October, 1914. The Allies attacked across the Flanders plain in Belgium, an area which provided very little natural cover and had an abnormally high sub-soil water level so that trenches became flooded soon after they were dug. The offensive, abandoned after seven weeks of bitter fighting, had only resulted in an insignificant advance. By then the BEF was showing signs of complete exhaustion and had suffered casualties far in excess of those which had been foreseen by the General Staff when the Flanders offensive was being prepared. One Division had lost 45% of its officers and 37% of its other ranks.[5] The indeterminate struggle was still in progress at the end of the year, at which time, according to the official history of the campaign, "The old British Army was gone beyond recall".[6]

The first British soldiers suffering from war neurosis started returning to England in September, 1914. Many of them were regarded as insane, but as no special arrangements had been made for their reception and treatment they were sent to ordinary military hospitals.[7] It was believed at their time that their brains had been damaged by blast-concussion from exploding shells, as it was not yet realized that war neurosis was primarily a psychological disorder.[8] It was in accordance with such a mistaken assumption that Charles S. Myers, a doctor in the Royal Army Medical Corps, described the condition for the first time by the name of "shell-shock" at the beginning of 1915.[9] Myers had seen his first shell-shock case in December, 1914, at a military hospital in Boulogne. The victim was a soldier who had been trapped in a barbed-wire entanglement during a spell of heavy German shelling. Myers said:

> Immediately after one of the shells had burst in front of him his sight became blurred. Another shell which then burst behind him gave him a greater shock – like a punch on the head, without any pain afterwards.

The soldier was not wounded but he was found to be suffering from a restricted field of vision and a loss of the functions of taste and smell.[10]

Around this time the *British Medical Journal* published an article by an RAMC doctor, who was attached to a military hospital in France, about the possible after-effects on soldiers in the vicinity of exploding shells, even though they had remained uninjured. They were liable, he said, to become blind, deaf or paralysed, and they might develop violent tremors of the body which could last for several days. He attributed these symptoms to hysterical and neurasthenic breakdowns.[11]

During the early years of the 20th century most nervous complaints were diagnosed as being either "hysteria" or "neurasthenia". In 1910 T.R. Glynn, a consultant neurologist and the Professor of Medicine at Liverpool University, wrote an article for *The Lancet* in which he analysed in detail the recognized forms of traumatic neurosis. Many of the symptoms he described were similar to those which in former years had been ascribed to nostalgia and windage. The principal characteristic of neurasthenia, he said, whether it occurred alone or in association with hysteria, was a sensation of pressure, emptiness, or other abnormal feelings. This was often accompanied by a stiffness which hampered all free movements. The patient also suffered from insomnia. "There may be difficulty in falling asleep, or sleep may more or less readily set in, but pass off in an hour or two, leaving the individual a prey to insufferable restlessness or fidgetiness and aggravated tinglings in the limbs."[12]

Dr Glynn said that the mental troubles which accompanied neurasthenia were many and marked. "On the emotional side there are sadness, weariness and pessimism; repugnance to effort, abnormal irritability, defective control of temper, tendency to weep on slight provocation, and timidity. On the intellectual side, lessened power of attention, defective memory and will power." In severe cases the patients looked dejected and stupid; their gait and movements were sluggish, and their speech was slow and halting.[13]

The number of soldiers in the BEF who were breaking down under the conditions of battle during the first few months of the war was causing concern both to the medical authorities and to the general public. On 12 December, 1914, an editorial in *The Lancet* commented:

It is no doubt somewhat early in the day to attempt to draw conclusions of wide applicability as to any connexion between the stress and strain of the war and the development of hysteria, neurasthenia, traumatic psycho-neurosis, and so on. Nevertheless, those who are coming in contact with the nervous side of the cases retired from the war are beginning to notice the frequency with which hysteria, traumatic and otherwise, is showing itself, not only among the Belgians but also in officers and men of our own forces.[14]

The editorial went on to cite some examples. Two Belgian soldiers had been in the vicinity of exploding shells. One of them was hit by a flying piece of wood and the other was buried under a pile of rubble. Neither had sustained any serious physical injury but both had developed paralysed limbs, due to hysteria, after the explosions. Two British officers had also been affected by hysterical paralysis. The first had been in hospital recovering from dysentery when his legs had suddenly become weak and painful. The second, a few days after leaving the front line to be treated for back-strain, had found that he was dragging his right foot and had partially lost the use of his right arm. All four of these men had formerly been in excellent physical condition and none of them had suffered from any nervous ailments in their past lives. The editorial speculated whether the rigours of the campaign might have affected them more than had been imagined and that, as a result, one particular incident in each of their cases might have given rise to their hysterical conditions. Even though the probability of self-suggestion must be considered.

The question remains whether physical factors such as fatigue, hunger, the strain of responsibility and constant attention to the organs of special sense, repeated air concussion from high explosives, and so on, in some unrecognised fashion so impress the nervous system of those who were apparently entirely normal, as to pave the way for the action of such a force as auto-suggestion. It is a matter at least, for serious discussion . . . It would be a mistake to conclude hastily from insufficient data, but in this connexion also there is matter for fruitful investigation at a later stage.[15]

The term "shell-shock" was soon adopted by the War Office in London as a diagnostic classification for all neuroses suffered by officers and men in the British forces which had been caused by their experiences in battle.[16] An American physician John T. MacCurdy, who made a study of shell-shock on the Western Front, described the typical symptoms of the condition. "The face of the patient is drawn," he said, "showing signs of fatigue, while emotional strain is exhibited by chronic frowning with considerable wrinkling of the forehead." The soldiers he examined looked as though they were under a great strain and could only maintain control over themselves with considerable effort. Their expressions denoted mental anguish rather than physical pain, and occasionally they had nervous mannerisms such as blinking or grimacing, "accompanied by a withdrawal of the head, suggesting the starting back from something unpleasant". A frequent complication was depression, taking the form of a feeling of hopelessness and shame for their own incompetence and cowardice. Sometimes this depression concluded with obsessive thoughts about the horrors they had seen on the battle-field and the horrors of war in general.[17]

Some of the shell-shock patients seen by Dr MacCurdy were suffering from conversion hysteria. This usually resulted in loss of speech, the development of a stammer, deafness, or paralysis of one or more limbs. Blindness sometimes occurred but it was more infrequent.[18]

Dr MacCurdy mentioned that the nightmares which afflicted shell-shocked men were often set against a normal, peacetime background. For instance, they would be pursuing their ordinary daily lives and would suddenly be confronted by the appearance of German soldiers armed with bayonets and bombs.[19] Dr T.A. Ross, whose book on war neuroses was published during the Second World War, thought that the worst of the nightmares were based on the patients' actual recollections of battle. Some of them dreaded to go to sleep, he wrote,

> because of the vivid dreams of a loathsome kind, which were almost worse than any experience they had gone through at the front. They would dream they were back in a trench being shelled. Dead friends would grin at them. Rats would emerge from the body-cavities of corpses. The air would be filled with the shriek and explosion of shells, and they waken with a scream, shaking and sweating. Some of them would leap out of their beds and hide under them.[20]

In the early part of the war it was considered a disgrace for a man to go sick with shell-shock. However, some of the doctors who were dealing with the victims did appreciate even then that war neurosis was a psychological disorder which did not necessarily emanate from cowardice. Dr MacCurdy believed that soldiers could be affected by their aversion to bloodshed. "There are probably no more fervent pacifists in existence," he stated, "than many of the men who are conscientiously fighting day after day."[21]

In August, 1914, the Germans were so convinced that their Army would be victorious within a maximum period of three months that they made no provisions for the treatment of soldiers suffering from war neurosis – in fact, their medical facilities were even inadequate for the reception of the large numbers of wounded troops returning from the front. Dr Clarence Neymann, a young American psychiatrist, was working in Germany when the war began and he immediately joined the German Red Cross. He was posted to the Heidelberg University Clinic which had been converted into a military base hospital. In November, 1914, and in subsequent months, said Dr Neymann, hardly a convoy of sick and wounded arrived at Heidelberg which did not include a number of "mental cases". These war neurotics were considered a great nuisance at base hospitals and nobody took much interest in them. As soon as possible they would be transferred to evacuation hospitals, virtually convalescent homes, where they "stagnated" for a while before being sent back to the front. Once they were in action again their neurotic symptoms invariably re-occurred and they had to be returned to base hospitals. This routine became so absurd that the military authorities attached a permanent or a visiting psychiatrist to every base hospital, and issued strict instructions that more care should be taken before patients with nervous disorders were posted back to the trenches. After that the situation improved considerably. Shell-shocked soldiers, on being discharged from hospital, were sent home for a rest and then were assigned to garrison duties near their home towns. If they were considered to be insane, or had paralysed limbs, they were admitted to the appropriate state institutions. Malingerers were posted to labour battalions far away from their homes.[22]

One type of war neurosis stood out among the rest, said Dr Neymann. It was called "*granatfieber*" – grenade fever. Patients affected with it appeared comparatively normal for most of the time, except that they complained of headaches, backaches and indigestion. However, if anyone spoke of conditions at the front, especially if grenades were mentioned, then,

> they immediately grew pale, trembled and in some cases so far lost control of their legs that they fell down. After such an experience they were restless and nervous and could not sleep without hypnotics for a number of days.[23]

On the outbreak of war the French Government had invited Dr Vaillard, the Medical Inspector of the French Army, and Professor Gilbert Ballet, a leading neurologist, to investigate whether the strain of warfare was likely to lead to the production of nervous disorders and insanity among soldiers, and, if necessary, to propose a remedy. As a result of their inquiry they reported, with misguided optimism, that the amount of insanity caused by the war would be inconsiderable, and that cases of mental disorder among men worn out by the fatigue of a campaign were extremely rare. They admitted that a certain number of conscripted French troops had suffered from delirium, but this had been put down to the after-effects of alcohol; as a result of them celebrating their mobilization "rather too joyously". Almost all of them had recovered sufficiently to be sent to the front.[24]

Chapter 8

During 1915 the BEF was being reinforced, for the most part, by ill-prepared soldiers from the Territorial Army and by Kitchener volunteers. After a few months training these men, straight from their civilian occupations, were pitched precipitately into the horrific conditions of the front line.

On 2 January, 1915, Lord Kitchener in a letter to General Sir John French, the Commander-in-Chief of the BEF, expressed a view which was destined to dominate the sterile thinking of the High Command for the next three years. He said:

> I suppose we must now recognize that the French Army cannot make a sufficient break through the German lines to bring about a retreat of the German forces from Northern Belgium. If that is so, the German lines in France may be looked upon as a fortress that cannot be carried by assault and that cannot be completely invested, with the result that the lines may be held by an investing force whilst operations proceed elsewhere.[1]

During the early months of the year the weather in Flanders was said to be the worst in living memory and the continued rain and snow caused severe flooding in the trenches, which were usually knee-deep in mud and water. The whole of the flat countryside was soaked in mud like a sponge, commented a lieutenant in the Seaforth Highlanders. The opposing trenches were very close together – in some places they were only twenty yards apart, he went on, "and there we sit facing each other and killing each other by every possible means."[2]

Even without direct offensive action, the shelling and sniping were exacting a steady toll of casualties on both sides.

In March, 1915, when the surface of the earth had been temporarily hardened by frost, Sir John French launched an offensive in the area of Neuve Chapelle. Although it was moderately successful, the BEF paid a heavy price for their modest gains of territory. It was a particularly harrowing experience for the new recruits: the concentration of exploding shells and mortar bombs as they left the cover of their trenches; the bayonet charge across no-man's-land through a hail of rifle and machine-gun bullets; and the sight of the dead, the dying and the wounded. A young trooper of the Yeomanry had occasion to pass among the casualties waiting for ambulances behind the line. There were men who had lost their arms, he said, and their clothes were soaked in blood. "I wanted to be sick," he added, "seeing all these poor buggers, some of them with their faces bashed and all. You never saw anything like it. It frightened me to death."[3].

The Second Battle of Ypres lasted from the end of April until the end of May, with continuous attacks and counter-attacks by both sides, but with no appreciable results. A German officer described the setting in which the soldiers were fighting:

> The whole countryside is yellow. The battlefield is fearful. A curious sour, heavy, penetrating smell of dead bodies strikes one . . . Bodies of cows and pigs lie, half decayed; splintered trees, the stumps of avenues; shell crater after shell crater on the roads and in the fields.[4]

About this time the Germans added a new horror to the weaponry of modern warfare – poison gas. They used it first in an attack against the French positions south of Ypres. It appeared as a greenish-yellow cloud drifting across no-man's-land and presently enveloping the French troops in a choking, lethal haze. Those who were not asphyxiated abandoned their trenches and staggered to the rear. Liddell Hart has said that British officers in the vicinity saw "a torrent of terrified humanity pouring backwards coughing and pointing to their throats as they fled".[5]

All through the months of April and May Britain's civilian-army was being grounded in the horrifying realities of the battlefield. An infantry major who took part in one of the innumerable succession of abortive attacks on the German positions around Ypres said that directly the troops had emerged from their trenches and began to advance they were "absolutely mown down" by shells and bullets. "The slaughter was cruel," he continued. "All across the shallow valley the dead and the dying were tossed into the air and dropped in mangled heaps."[6] A lance-corporal in a Territorial battalion which had only just joined the BEF told how he and several others were lying behind a hedge when a shell exploded near them and two men had both of their legs blown off. "One lived a few minutes," he said, "the other lived about half-an-hour."[7]

A soldier soon becomes used to the sight of dead bodies, but he seldom grows accustomed to the sight of the hideously wounded. An orderly in a Casualty Clearing Station described a man being carried in with his face covered by a bandage. "When the bandage was off," he said, "we saw the man had no eyes, no nose, no chin, no mouth – and he was alive." The doctor-in-charge told the orderly to give him four times the usual dose of morphine. This achieved the obvious intention and the man died.[8]

People at home in Britain were mystified by "the strange malady" which was affecting more and more troops in the BEF, and was variously described as "shell-shock", "nervous breakdown", "collapse", "neurasthenia", "traumatic hysteria" or "malingering". In the early months of 1915 it seemed to be so prevalent that it was almost reaching the proportions of an epidemic.[9] The civil population found it all the more puzzling because for many years past British education had centred on, and had extolled, the cultivation of "character", implying as it did the rigorous control of a person's thoughts and actions.[10]

Lord Moran, despite the fact that he had served as a regimental medical officer on the Western Front, typified this viewpoint in a study of courage in action which he wrote after the war had ended, and in which he said, "I contend that fortitude in war has its root in morality . . . and that war itself is but one more test – the supreme test, if you will – of character."[11]

At the beginning of 1915 the War Office instructed Lieut–Colonel W.A. Turner, a consultant neurologist then serving in the RAMC, to report on the increasing number of men in the British Forces who were affected with mental and nervous illnesses, and to make recommendations as to the conditions under which they should be treated.[12] Dr Turner spent three months at base hospitals in France conducting his investigations and he described some of the cases he had seen in an article published in the *British Medical Journal* after his return to England.[13] The patients were mostly young, he said, the majority being only 22 or 23. Their condition had been caused, in his view, either by their proximity to shell explosions, or by nervous exhaustion due to physical strain, sleeplessness and other stressful circumstances associated with the campaign.

Before a casualty reached the base hospital he passed through his Regimental Aid Post, where he was treated by the battalion medical officer, and the Casualty Clearing Station, at which he was classified and, if necessary, received emergency attention before being sent back to the base. Some of the men with shattered nerves, said Dr Turner, came to the Casualty Clearing Station in a state of mental stupor; others more severely affected were entirely "unconscious of their surroundings". On his admission to a base hospital the shell-shock patient would immediately curl up under the bedclothes and "from time to time he would look out, as though peering over the parapet of a trench, stare wildly around him, and hide under the clothes again". One of the men used to sit up in bed suddenly and then cry out "He's gone! He's gone!" It was discovered later that his brother had been killed while standing beside him in a trench.[14]

In Dr Turner's opinion many of the patients he saw were still in a state of "hysterical stupor" and seemed to be endlessly re-living a past terrifying experience at the front. Some of them were suffering from deaf-mutism; others from loss of memory, blindness, or neurasthenia. The worst of the cases were being sent back to England, but those less severely affected frequently recovered after a short rest and were returned to duty.[15]

At the end of March, 1915, Charles S. Myers, another RAMC officer, was appointed to replace Dr Turner as Consultant Neurologist to the War Office. Among his other duties, he was required to visit the base hospitals in France and "to select suitable cases of nervous or mental shock and neurasthenia for transference to appropriate institutions in England for treatment". At that time there were no special military hospitals in France for the reception of the shell-shocked who were still referred to as "mental cases". Myers decided to set up a separate mental ward at the base hospital in Boulogne where he could make his final selection of the patients who should be sent back to England.[16]

The only available accommodation for the Mental Ward in Boulogne was the attic floor at the top of a large building which had recently been constructed as a hotel, but before its opening had been converted into a General Hospital. The ward, said Myers, was dismal, ill-ventilated and over-crowded. The miserable conditions were not the only factor which hampered Myer's original purpose. The Army medical authorities, adopting a slightly cynical attitude, started to send to the Mental Ward three other categories of patients as well as the severe shell-shock cases. These were the men who had become insane, suspected epileptics and prisoners who had been convicted at courts martial but were awaiting reports concerning the soundness of their minds. Myers continued to protest about this unintended use of the ward, particularly about prisoners being sent there. "It seemed to me undesirable," he said, "that innocent men who had mentally broken down under the strain of warfare should be so closely associated with those accused and convicted of such offences as murder, attempted suicide, theft or desertion."[17]

Many of the severely shell-shocked patients at Boulogne were fearful that if they were sent back to England they would be dispatched to lunatic asylums.[18] In fact the medical services in England were ill-prepared to receive an influx of mentally-damaged casualties from the BEF. This was recognized in a leading article in *The Lancet* on 1 May, 1915, which stated, "The problems of dealing with cases of nervous and mental disorders in soldiers on active service has become at the present day a matter of serious difficulty and of considerable practical importance."[19]

Shell-shock patients arriving in England from France early in 1915 were sent straightaway to a clearing hospital, either the Royal Victoria Hospital at Netley or the 4th London General Hospital at Denmark Hill. A number of patients complained about the harsh treatment and the uncomfortable conditions to which they had been subjected in France, and some of those suffering from paralysis alleged that they had been tortured with electric shocks.[20] From the clearing hospitals they were passed to some London hospital which specialized in nervous diseases or to one of the institutions recently taken over by the military authorities for use as hospitals, most of which had previously been lunatic asylums. Soldiers who were transferred to these institutions feared that they would be regarded as insane for the rest of their lives.[21]

Relatives and friends of the shell-shocked soldiers who had been returned to England were extremely concerned that they might be certified by the Lunacy Board and indefinitely confined in asylums.[22] In order to dispel their anxiety the Government introduced the Mental Health Bill, 1915, which provided that any patient undergoing treatment for "a mental disorder of recent origin, arising from wounds, shock, or from other causes connected with the war" could remain at a hospital or institution for a period of up to six months without being certified insane.[23] The intention seems to have been any soldier who could not be cured within six months must be certified.

The recognized treatment for shell-shock during the first year of the war was to keep the patient in conditions of quiet, rest and relaxation. Dr Wilfred Harris, whose book on nerve injuries and shock was published in the summer of 1915, believed that the prognosis for most of the men was favourable. "With proper methods of suggestive treatment," he wrote, "the cases of nervous shock can nearly all be rapidly or even immediately cured."[24] Some doctors had a theory that the best results could be achieved by inducing their patients, under hypnosis, to re-create the events which had led directly to their breakdown. Dr W. Brown was an exponent of this method. With his patient lying on a couch in a hypnotic sleep, he would say, "The moment you feel my hand on your forehead you will be back in the trenches, and you will live again your frightening experiences." Dr Brown would then touch the recumbent man on the forehead and the process of subconscious recollection would begin. By releasing the patient's half-hidden terrors into his sentient thoughts, it was supposed to cure him of his neurosis.[25]

Lord Knutsford, a philanthropist and hospital reformer, founded four private hospitals during the year 1915 for officers suffering from war neurosis, principally to spare them from being placed in mental institutions. The first of these was opened in January "for the observation and treatment of officers who had been rendered

54

incapable of service by the stress of warfare and the horrors of the trenches". It was in a large London private house in Palace Green, close to Kensington Gardens. The accommodation and regime were described in an article in *The Lancet*.[26] There were thirty-three single bedrooms, each of which had "plain grey walls with no pictures or ornaments or anything else to attract or distract the attention of the tired men, to whom complete and absolute rest of the body and mind is the first essential of recovery." The officers had all their meals alone in their rooms except for afternoon tea. They were allowed out for one short, solitary walk in Kensington Gardens every day. Little or no active treatment was given at the hospital, apart from the occasional use of massage, electric shocks, or suggestive therapy, which took the form of "explaining to the patient the mechanism of his retarded mental processes". On average, officers remained in this atmosphere of monastic seclusion for between three and four weeks before moving on to Hospital No. 2.

The second Knutsford Hospital, opened in April, 1915, was a convalescent home for officers who had passed through the first hospital. It was in a comfortable private house with a spacious garden in Campden Hill, a fashionable area of London. There was accommodation for thirty patients, who again had separate bedrooms. The conditions, according to the *Lancet* article, were very different from those at Palace Green, as the "note of austerity" was entirely missing. The officers took their meals together in their own Mess, and they could relax in well-furnished sitting-rooms with beautiful pictures on the walls, where they were able to refresh their "reviving brains". If they wished, they could play billiards or croquet. The patients remained at this hospital for about six weeks before they were considered to be sufficiently cured to return to the front.[27]

The third and fourth of the Knutsford Special Hospitals for Officers were opened later in the year. The third was intended for patients who had developed shell-shock as a result of being wounded and the fourth was for "definite cases of mental disorder".[28]

The British Army did not accept the actuality of shell-shock, nor was it regarded as a valid defence in courts martial for cowardice or desertion in the field. It was virtually useless for a man to plead, in answer to a charge of desertion, that he had been suffering from amnesia. A private in the King's Own Scottish Borderers, a regular soldier aged 20, went absent from the trenches in the Ypres Salient on 1 March, 1915. He remain at liberty for four months before being arrested by the Military Police. His Commanding Officer described him at his court martial as being "a well-behaved man, but not a particularly intelligent one," who had served with the battalion since they came to France the previous August. In his defence the private said that he did not know why he had left the trench. They were being heavily bombarded at the time and he had lost his memory. He was sentenced to death and shot without undergoing any medical examination.[29] A 21-year-old private in the Royal West Kent Regiment, at his court martial for desertion in June, 1915, claimed that he had lost his memory as a result of his nerves being shattered by the sights he had seen on the battlefield. Again, he was not medically examined before his execution.[30]

Medical Boards were a rarity after a prisoner had been sentenced to death at a court martial. A private in the Worcester Regiment, who was convicted of desertion at the end of June, 1915, told the court that he had fractured his skull when he was 16 and it had affected his behaviour ever since. Arrangements were made for a Medical Board to examine him, but they were restricted to reporting on one specific point, namely "whether an injury, sustained nine years ago, has affected his memory". The findings of the Board were that, although the man had sustained an injury to his skull, there was no evidence that this had had a permanent affect on his nervous system or had caused him to lose his memory. The doctors had complied with their narrow instructions and had not gone on, apparently, to consider whether the soldier's memory might have been impaired for any other reason. He was shot at dawn a few days after his examination.[31]

Perhaps even the most favourable medical reports would not have saved many convicted soldiers from execution. A 20-year-old private in the Black Watch who had gone absent from the front line in January, 1916, was sentenced to death ten days later. A Medical Board reported on him:

Although not of unsound mind, he is suffering from a marked degree of neurasthenia. Whether this is the result of shell-shock or of recent onset, we are unable to say.

56

In spite of these findings by two Medical Officers, the man was shot by a firing squad at an abbatoir in Belgium.[32]

Even as late as May, 1916, said Colonel Myers, who was then the Consulting Psychologist to the Army, "From a military standpoint, a deserter was either 'insane' and destined for the 'mad house', or responsible and should be shot."[33]

Chapter 9

Throughout the summer of 1915 the opposing armies on the Western Front remained fairly static, but the shelling, the sniping, the patrolling and the localized attacks continued endlessly. The BEF was sustaining casualties at the rate of about three hundred a day. The gaps in the ranks were being filled, for the most part, with raw Kitchener volunteers, many of whom were in fact too young or too old for active service and had only managed to enlist by lying about their ages. The author Robert Graves, who was serving in France as an infantry officer at the time, said some of the new recruits in his platoon were men over 40, and some were youths of less than 18.[1]

The troops in the trenches were perpetually debilitated through lack of sleep, yet under the Army Act of 1914 sleeping on the post was still a capital offence. A corporal in the Durham Light Infantry admitted that he had dozed off while standing with his arms folded on the parapet. "From my diary," he said, "I could prove that the men had been allowed twenty-two hours sleep in eight days." When his battalion was relieved from the line he had been surprised to find that he could hardly walk. Ironically, he was due to attend an inquiry into pending charges of "sleeping on post" against several members of his platoon, but most of them had been killed or wounded so the inquiry was cancelled.[2] According to a sergeant in the Gordon Highlanders, he and his men did not have more than two hours sleep at a time for four successive days. He added, "There were a lot of cases of shell-shock among the men who were more highly-strung."[3]

Meanwhile, the British medical profession, as a whole, had not yet realized the fact that war neurosis was largely a psychological disorder. On 14 August, 1915, *The Lancet* published an editorial under the heading, "Nervous Manifestations Due to the Wind of High Explosives." It began, "The possibility of injury due to 'the wind of the bullet' has long been recognized," and went on to say that the much more injurious wind of an explosion did not seem to have received due attention and had been neglected in the diagnosis of hysteria. The anonymous writer mentioned the case of a soldier being affected by paraplegia at the Front in November, 1914. Another, in March 1915, was paralysed down one side of his body and lost the ability to speak. A second soldier in March, 1915, became "almost comatosed" and went deaf in one ear. The editorial finished:

> It would be contradictory to expect the human organism to be
> unaffected by violent explosions which produce such an effect
> on surrounding objects, animate and inanimate.[4]

Medical opinion in France at this time seems to have been equally mystified in regard to the way some soldiers were affected by their proximity to exploding shells. It was reported that three French neurologists, at a meeting in Paris, had provided evidence of shell explosions causing grave nervous symptoms. This, they contended, raised the question whether the patients were suffering from hysteria, or if they had sustained some actual physical damage.[5]

Men in the line were fully aware that shell explosions were by no means either the only or the main causes of war neurosis. In the library of the Wellcome Institute for the History of Medicine there is an anonymous account by an officer, probably a captain, of a nervous breakdown he suffered in July, 1915.[6] During the three months of the Second Battle of Ypres, he said, his battalion had extremely heavy casualties and on three occasions he had been the senior surviving officer. "After the third time in June," he continued, "I knew I was approaching the end of my tether." He had been sent on special home leave for ten days, and had arrived back in France at the beginning of July, just before his battalion was to take part in another attack. They succeeded in capturing three lines of enemy trenches with relatively small losses and took over the German reserve trench as their new front line. For the next two days and nights they were subjected to intensive shelling – "the most terrific fire" he had ever encountered, he said, which had devastated the trench and almost wiped out the

59

battalion. On the second evening the seven remaining officers met together in a dug-out to consider the seriousness of the situation. While the discussion was taking place an enemy shell scored a direct hit on the dugout, killing three of the officers and seriously wounding three of the others. Once again the narrator was left to take over the remnants of the battalion. "The fact that I was responsible and in charge," he said, "saved my reason for the time being."

Having arranged for the evacuation of the wounded and the distribution of rations and ammunition, he had retired to an empty dugout where he had drunk three-quarters of a tumbler of neat whisky. Eventually his battalion was relieved and he had collected his men and marched them back to the rear lines. On the way they were met by their Quartermaster who, oblivious of the extent of their casualties, had brought up all the officers' horses for them to ride. The narrator says:

> When I saw the horses and realized what had happened, it finished me. I broke down, and I don't mind telling you, I cried for a week.

After the war had lasted for a year with no realistic prospect of its ending a number of people in Britain were troubled about the welfare of the shell-shocked patients who were being sent home from the base hospitals in France. On 21 September, 1915, the Under-Secretary for War stated at Question Time in the House of Commons that "military mental and nervous cases" were treated in the neurological wards in twenty-three military hospitals in the United Kingdom. They were also being sent to the Springfield House Hospital in Wandsworth and the Red Cross Hospital at Maghull near Liverpool.[7]

Up to this, soldiers suffering from shell-shock had remained in the Army while they were undergoing treatment, but it was rumoured that some of them were going to be discharged as unfit and transferred to the care of the Lunacy Commissioners. In reply to a question on 22 September the Under-Secretary for War admitted that "the subject of the disposal of the more serious mental cases has been receiving consideration and had caused the authorities considerable anxiety". He said that in view of the increasing number of incurable cases it would be impossible to continue the existing system indefinitely. From then on any shell-shocked soldiers with general paralysis, chronic

60

epilepsy or chronic insanity "would be dealt with in the manner laid down in paragraphs 403, 404, and 408 of King's Regulations".[8] He did not elaborate further and he was not pressed for clarification of his reply. In fact, the paragraphs of King's Regulations to which he referred only applied to the procedures for removing or discharging a "lunatic soldier". If it had been decided to remove him to an asylum for temporary treatment, it was necessary to obtain a reception order for him in accordance with the provisions of the Lunacy Act, 1890. When the lunatic soldier was going to be discharged from the Army, provided he was not dangerous to himself or to the public, enquiries had to be made to ascertain whether his friends would be willing to receive him. If they declined, he was to be handed over to the charge of his parish authorities. However, if he was a "dangerous lunatic" the case could not be disposed of until the appropriate form for the admission of dangerous lunatics to asylums had been drawn up and processed.[9]

The Battle of Loos began a few days after the Under-Secretary for War had made these statements in the House of Commons. Neither Sir John French nor his senior commanders wished to carry out an offensive on this particular part of the front, which they considered too flat and lacking in cover, but they had yielded to pressure from General Joffre, the French Commander-in-Chief, and from their own War Minister, Lord Kitchener. The attack was launched on the morning of 26 September between Loos and La Bassée by 75,000 troops from six totally inexperienced Divisions. Liddell Hart has said:

> Never, surely, were novice Divisions thrown into a vital stroke
> in a more difficult or absurd manner, and in an atmosphere of
> greater misconception of the situation in all quarters.[10]

The attack was a failure, for all the courage that was shown by the Territorial Army battalions and the Kitchener volunteers. The advances made were insignificant; the losses were immense.

It was a terrifying experience for the assaulting infantry, most of whom were taking part in their first bayonet charge. A sergeant in the Northumberland Fusiliers has described how the Germans allowed his battalion to get well into no-man's-land before suddenly opening up with their machine guns. Then, he said, "Men were just mown down. It was just slaughter, all hell let loose. Men began to stumble and fall, and machine guns were firing from the front of us and enfilading from the left hand side."[11] A private in the London Scottish, attacking in another sector of the line, said, "The chap in front of me had the whole of his face blown away. I've never seen anything so horrible in my life. It was just a red mass, his face. He sank down moaning, making a terrible noise, and I had to push on."[12]

After the battle came the appalling task of clearing away the dead. Years later a soldier who had fought at Loos recalled the scene. It was impossible to bury all the corpses, he said. Men lay where they had fallen. Sometimes earth had been slung on top of them, but the rain washed most of it away and "you'd see a boot or a puttee sticking out, or an arm or a hand, sometimes faces . . . the stench was terrible because of all that rotting flesh."[13]

The Battle of Loos was protracted until the beginning of November when the onset of wintry weather ruled out the possibility of renewing the offensive. General Sir William Robertson, who was the Chief of Staff in France in 1915, endeavoured to justify the costly failure of Loos by claiming that, although the operations were "unproductive of decisive success", they had furnished "useful experience in the handling of new troops." Winston Churchill, in his history of the First World War, has commented scathingly that this "useful experience" could be deemed an inadequate result from 95,000 British casualties.[14]

In December, 1915, Sir John French was replaced as Commander-in-Chief of the BEF by Sir Douglas Haig, who retained the position until the end of the war. Throughout his whole command, Churchill has written, Haig adhered to the belief that the only method of waging war on the Western Front was by wearing down the enemy and "killing Germans in a war of attrition". His policy had always been the same: "Gather together every man and gun, and wear down the enemy by constant and if possible by ceaseless attacks."[15]

The BEF had been condemned to spending another winter of immobility in the danger, discomfort and squalor of the trenches. A young infantry officer, Raymond Asquith, son of the British Prime Minister, described the conditions of the front line in a letter home. The trenches were filthy, he wrote, with mud and water over knee-deep, and the cold was intense. The Front Line was continually infested by plagues of rats "which gnaw the dead bodies and then run about on one's face making obscene noises and gestures".[16] And all the time there was the shelling and the small arms fire. This atmosphere, naturally, was conducive to the development of war neurosis and many soldiers broke down under the constant stress and strain.

Towards the end of the year the Army Council issued a directive that in future "shell-shock and shell-concussion cases" should have the letter "W" prefixed to their casualty-reports if their condition was due to enemy action: this would result in their being categorized as "wounded" and would entitle them to wear a wound stripe on their tunics.[17] It would seem to be obvious that the vast majority of men who broke down in the front line did so as a result of their battle experiences. Yet, according to Charles S. Myers, Regimental Medical Officers "almost invariably declined to diagnose cases of temporary (confused) insanity, due to mental shock or exhaustion, as 'shell-shock'. Instead, they preferred to classify the men either as 'Mental' or 'Mental?'"[18] In view of this, patients suffering from severe neuroses who should have been evacuated to England without any delay, were often kept in Casualty Clearing Stations while their units were contacted in an effort to find out whether or not they should be sent home with a "W" appended to their medical records. Until the matter had been finally decided the records were entered with the letters "NYDN", denoting that they were "Not Yet Diagnosed Nervous".[19]

The Allies began their ill-fated invasion of the Gallipoli peninsula in April, 1915. Throughout the sweltering summer and the bitterly cold months of the early winter, the expeditionary forces strove unsuccessfully to extend their bridgeheads, while the casualties mounted and the sickness increased. At the beginning of December it was decided to discontinue the wastage and to terminate the campaign.

Temporary Surgeon MacBean Ross, the Medical Officer of the 2nd Battalion of the Royal Marines, has described the conditions under which the doctors had to work after the landings at Gallipoli. The distance from the firing line to the beaches was only about five miles, he said, and the whole of the back area was open to shellfire. The forward Sick Bay, the Marines' equivalent to a Regimental Aid Post, was usually in a portion of a disused trench as close to the front line as possible. From here the casualty was passed back to the Sick Bay in the so-called "rest camp". This consisted of a small dugout which in the winter was protected from the elements by a covering of groundsheets, laced together to form a hood. In such locations as these they tended the wounded and the sick, who were often suffering from dysentery and typhoid.[20]

Dr MacBean Ross mentioned briefly the subject of "Mental Condition in Gallipoli". He said:

> The nervous strain of being under shellfire day after day, week after week, and month after month might be expected to cause a large amount of mental depression and even insanity amongst the troops. The expectation was not realized in this battalion.[21]

Other units were not so fortunate as the 2nd Royal Marines. The Ministry of Pensions statistics show that 159 officers and 1,725 other ranks from the Gallipoli Expeditionary Force were admitted to hospital suffering from "diseases of the nervous system" during the short campaign.[22]

The French and the British military authorities were equally worried about the number of men who were breaking down on the Western Front, and in 1915 they still shared the belief that the primary cause of the problem was the blast from exploding shells.

Professor André Léri, who was in charge of a large French Army Neurological Centre, divided his patients into two groups, the first suffering from a "commotional" and the second an "emotional" disorder. The commotional patients had escaped being wounded by a fragment of an exploding shell, but had been injured as a direct result of the explosion. For instance, the blast might have knocked them over or collapsed a dugout on top of them. They were usually brought to a field hospital, often on a stretcher, some hours or days after the occurrence. Léri maintained that their physical injuries, in such circumstances, had disturbed the nervous centres of their brains and caused them to develop neurasthenia – as sometimes happens, he said, to the victims of accidents in civilian life.[23]

The emotional type of patient, according to Léri, who had sustained some undetected wound from a shell explosion, rather than an apparent physical injury, was generally either inert or agitated when he arrived at the field hospital. He was always so fatigued that he had to be led to his bed and put into it. If he was woken up he moaned and became agitated. He looked up "with a bewildered air, his eyes wide open, haggard, as if he was the prey to some intense anxiety and some horrible vision". Later, he was affected by insomnia, and when he slept he had frequent nightmares, centreing on the incident which had caused him to break down. After a spell in hospital, said Léri, the majority of the emotional cases were considered to have recovered sufficiently to return to the Front.[24]

The German High Command and the German Army doctors were inclined to look on war neurosis as a violation of military discipline. At a meeting of the Berlin Medical Society in November, 1915, a doctor attached to an army hospital gave expression to this view. He told his audience that 50 per cent of the soldiers in his care suffered from neurasthenia. "Most of these patients," he said, "particularly the middle-aged, do not wish to recover, dreading a return to the Front." He suggested that radical measures were essential in order to prevent the army being deprived of the services of these men. In his view they should not be sent home, but should be kept at a convalescent quarters near to line, a procedure which was already being adopted on the Western Front. Another speaker agreed and said that the influence on the patients of their parents, their wives and their children was extremely detrimental.[25]

Shortly after this a Dr Kaufmann introduced a system of treatment for war neurotic German soldiers which even some of his colleagues condemned as being inhuman. Kaufmann relied on a combination of suggestion and painful electric shocks, aiming to cure the neurotic in one session. According to his own account of his methods, which he published in 1916, the treatment took place in an atmosphere of strict military discipline. "From the moment the patient was admitted to hospital he was impressed with the spirit of unquestioning, unreasoning obedience." He was warned immediately that although he was going to be hurt, the cure would be complete and permanent. He was then given a series of powerful electric shocks, "supplemented by vigorous word-suggestion". The process might continue for hours before the presiding physician was satisfied. Afterwards the patient would be kept in hospital for several weeks, both to recover from his ordeal and to diminish the chances of a relapse.[26]

After the war reports were current in Vienna that German and Austrian soldiers suffering from war neuroses had been brutally treated by Army doctors. The Austrian War Ministry set up an inquiry into the matter and invited Sigmund Freud to give evidence as an expert witness. Freud agreed to do so and submitted a memorandum on "The Electrical Treatment of War Neurotics".

In the course of a clear and reasoned document, Freud said that the form of treatment used by the German Army had borne a stigma from the very first. He went on:

> It did not aim at the patient's recovery, or not in the first instance; it aimed, above all, at restoring his fitness for service. Here Medicine was serving purposes foreign to its essence. The physician himself was under military command and had his own personal dangers to fear – loss of seniority or a charge of neglecting his duty – if he allowed himself to be led by considerations other than those prescribed for him. The insoluble conflict between the claims of humanity, which normally carry decisive weight for a physician, and the demands of a national war, was bound to confuse his activity.[27]

Although this form of treatment had proved to be successful, said Freud, its results were not lasting. It was based on a misconception, as only the smallest proportion of war neurotics were malingerers. The unconscious motive for the patient's symptoms was to escape from the war, but he was not aware of this. The pain of the electric current had been more intolerable than conditions at the Front, and just as he had "fled from the war into illness", the treatment had compelled him "to flee back from illness into health, that is so say, into fitness for active service". However, once he returned to the Front and found himself again under fire, his fear of the electric current receded, just as during the treatment his fear of active service had faded. Inevitably, his neurotic symptoms had returned and he had relapsed into a neurotic condition.[28]

In conclusion, Freud alleged that the Army doctors had sometimes increased the strength of the current "to an unbearable point" in order to deprive the war neurotics of the advantage they had gained from their illness. "The fact has never been contradicted," he said, "that in German hospitals there were deaths at the time during treatment, and suicides as a result of it."[29]

66

Chapter 10

By the end of 1915 the British Army had lost 21,747 officers and 490,673 other ranks, of whom approximately two-fifths were either killed or missing.

In the war of attrition which was then being waged on the Western Front there was a perpetual need for reinforcements to replace the casualties and to provide more formations for the line of battle. On 1 January, 1916, the strength of the BEF was 987,200 and many more new Divisions were being trained in England to take part in the next offensive. The manpower problem was becoming more and more acute. Already, according to the *Official History of the Campaign*, "the cream of the nation" had enlisted, and the supply of volunteer-recruits was rapidly coming to an end.[1]

In January, 1916, Parliament passed the Military Services Act which provided that all voluntary enlistment was to cease and that any man between the ages of 18 and 41, who was either unmarried or was a widower without dependants, was liable to be called up for general service with the armed forces. Four months later the provisions were extended to include married men in a similar age group.

A "special discussion" on shell-shock, organized by the Royal Society of Medicine, took place in London during the last week of January. A neurologist, Dr Henry Head, told the participants that shell-shock was in fact a heterogeneous collection of different nervous disorders ranging from concussion to sheer funk and the only feature they had in common was that in all of them the patients had lost control of their nerves. One speaker contended that the real causative agent of the disorder was shock, and a doctor who had analysed seventy cases of shell-shock said that those principally affected were

67

older NCOs who had undergone a prolonged period of stress and lack of sleep.[2]

The Lancet, which reported the special discussion, stated that those who took part were in general agreement that if explosions were of sufficient severity, shell-shock could be produced even on a previously healthy brain, and that a contributory factor, in some cases, was the inhalation of poisonous gases left behind in trenches and in dugouts after the explosion of a shell. However, opinions varied widely on the best method of treating the disorder.[3]

At this time shell-shock had become a subject of particular interest to the medical profession in Britain, and when Major Fred Mott was invited by the Medical Society of London to deliver the Lettsomian lectures for 1916 he chose as his subject "The Effects of High Explosives upon the Central Nervous System". Dr Mott, a neurologist, was regarded as an expert on the subject and was on the staff of the 4th London General Hospital which specialized in the treatment of shell-shocked soldiers. He gave the first of his lectures on 12 February. Apart from inflicting physical injuries, he told his audience, shellfire caused continuous anxious tension which, combined with the horrible sights of death and destruction in the front line, tended to exhaust, and eventually even to shatter, the strongest nervous system. He went on:

> To live in trenches or underground for days or weeks, exposed continually to wet, cold and often, owing to the shelling of the communication trenches, to hunger, combined with fearful tension and apprehension, may so lower the vital resistance of the strongest nervous system that a shell bursting near, and without causing any visible injury, is sufficient to lead to as sudden loss of consciousness.[4]

Even a sound soldier might acquire a neurasthenic condition in the front line, said Dr Mott, and if he was of a timorous or a neurotic disposition he would be less capable of withstanding the terrifying effects of shellfire and the stresses of trench warfare.[5]

In one of his subsequent Lettsomian lectures Dr Mott outlined the more common symptoms of shell-shock. Patients frequently suffered from speech defects; sometimes they were completely dumb, sometimes they stammered or stuttered. The ability to hear, like the ability to speak, might be totally lost, and vision could be greatly impaired. Many patients were affected with paralysis, usually with paraplegia, although they might only be paralysed down one side of their bodies. Patients often complained of palpitation and breathlessness on exertion, or else of sensory disturbances.[6]

As a rule soldiers with shell-shock were suffering no pain when they were first admitted to hospital, said Dr Mott, because they were in a heavy and dazed condition. But later, as their consciousness became less clouded, they were invariably afflicted with excruciating headaches. In addition, they were tormented by the terrifying dreams which beset them during the night or when they were half awake.[7]

Dr Mott spoke with approval about the decision of the War Office to recognize shell-shock as a definite type of war injury from the point of view of pensions or compensation. However, he said that it was difficult in many cases for doctors to detect whether a soldier was really shell-shocked or was just malingering. Often one had to rely upon the statements made by the patient himself about the onset and nature of his conditions, and even if he was genuine he might well have undergone a period of amnesia and be unable to provide any details.[8]

A week after Dr Mott had delivered the last of his three Lettsomian Lectures, *The Lancet* commented in an editorial that his views would be studied with interest, as the dire results of the use of high explosives had been a matter of concern since the early days of the war. The military authorities had been subjected to a formidable campaign of invective for treating soldiers with nervous symptoms as though they were all insane or else were malingering. It had been assumed too hastily that these men would either be certified as lunatics or returned to duty, or that they would be discharged from the Army with inadequate pensions. Questions had been asked in Parliament and letters had been written to the press about the matter. Public anxiety had been somewhat allayed when many of these cases were described as "neurasthenia", and by the introduction of the new term "shell-shock", indicating the cause of the disorder without attempting any further clarification. The sudden appearance of all or some of the symptoms in healthy young males had given a new impetus to research. It had once been believed that shell-shock patients could be divided into two classes; firstly, those who had a pre-existing form of mental deficiency, and secondly, those who were exhibiting a type of hysterical manifestation. Recent study had revealed that this theory was fallacious. The editorial ended:

> It is not so clear, however, that the keenest investigation had yet supplied a satisfactory answer to all the doubts which have been expressed.[9]

The new glimmer of enlightenment with regard to shell-shock had not permeated to the official thinking in the BEF.

There was a traditional view in the British Army that Medical Officers were callous and uncompassionate, suspecting every sick soldier of being a malingerer. Dr Harold Dearden, who served as an MO on the Western Front, admitted that most MOs were out to prove that nothing whatsoever was wrong with the men who reported sick, especially when their units were in or near the trenches.[10] On one occasion Dearden was called as a witness at the court-martial of a soldier who had deserted from the front line. In Dearden's opinion the man was "a pitiful degenerate", and he recorded in his diary:

> I went to the trial determined to give him no help of any sort, for I detest his type; and seeing so many good fellows go out during the night's shelling made me all the more bitter against him for trying to back down. I really hoped he would be shot, as indeed was anticipated by all of us.[11]

Some MOs were more understanding about the stresses endured by the infantry in the trenches. Another regimental doctor, Lord Moran, spoke of troops coming back from the line looking tired and ill. "The very gait of these men has lost its spring," he said, "The sap had gone out of them. They are dried up."[12]

The inability of Medical Officers and of the members of courts martial to appreciate the effects of war neurosis probably resulted in a number of morally innocent soldiers being shot at dawn. A 21-year-old private in the Middlesex Regiment was tried for desertion on 4 March, 1916. Three weeks before, when his battalion had been in the front line, he had reported to his CQMS that a grenade had exploded near him and he was still suffering from shock. The CQMS formed the

70

impression that he was in a nervous condition, but the MO disagreed and found him fit for duty. Instead of returning to the trenches the man had deserted. Although he bore a good character he was sentenced to death and executed.[13]

A private in the East Kent Regiment, who was sentenced to death for desertion on 4 April, 1916, had pleaded unsuccessfully with his company commander to be excused from duty in the line because he could not stand any more shelling and his nerves had been completely shattered.[14] If a soldier cracked up under the strains of battle even his courage in the past did not always save him from execution. A private in the Royal Fusiliers was court-martialled for desertion on 20 May, 1916. His Acting Company Sergeant-Major, giving character evidence, said that he had proved himself to be one of the best men in the company, and was constantly volunteering for patrols and for other dangerous jobs. The man's Commanding Officer added his opinion that "up to the time of this offence he was always reckoned a good and plucky soldier". The accused private told the court that he did not know why he had deserted and that he had "suffered with his head ever since". It was not considered necessary for him to undergo a medical examination before he was sentenced to death and shot.[15]

A medical report on an accused soldier at a capital court martial might well be ignored in deciding whether or not he should be executed. A 26-year-old miner from Derbyshire, serving as a private in the Northumberland Fusiliers, was tried for desertion on 28 April, 1916. He had said in evidence that his brother had died in a lunatic asylum, his sister suffered from fits and he had been told by his doctor at home that he himself had something wrong with his head. A lieutenant, acting as defence advocate, had then intervened to say that the accused, to whom he had first spoken half an hour before the trial had started, was anxious that his own doctor should be called as a witness. In spite of this, the case continued without an adjournment. The only medical evidence placed before the court was a report by a Captain in the RAMC who stated that, although he had discovered nothing to show that the prisoner was not responsible for his actions, if an examination by lunacy specialists were to take place "a more definite diagnosis could be arrived at". The suggestion was ignored and the miner was sentenced to death. The Divisional Commander was worried about the trial, and he recommended that further

71

enquiries should be made before the man was shot. However, General Sir Douglas Haig, the Commander-in-Chief, disagreed. Apparently he believed that there were sufficient medical details in the file already and he confirmed the death sentence without delaying the matter any further.[16]

A short while before this soldier was sentenced to death, concern had been expressed publicly by an authority on shell-shock about the recruitment for the forces of mentally unstable men. On 15 April, 1916 *The Lancet* had published an article, "Shock and the Soldier" by Professor G. Elliott Smith, Dean of the Faculty of Medicine at Manchester University and a consultant at Moss Side Hospital. He began by saying that the manifold problems relating to soldiers suffering from what was designated by "the vague and non-committal term 'shock'" were urgently calling for full consideration. In the selection of recruits, people with certain physical complaints were automatically rejected, but no measures were taken "to exclude the mental weakling whose failure might lead to infinitely graver consequences, not merely to himself but to the whole of his unit.[17]

Professor Elliott Smith also criticized the custom of returning men to the firing line after they had had nervous breakdowns. It had already been proved that they were useless as combatants and once they were at the Front again they would almost certainly succumb at the first strain. He went on:

> There is no class of patients in the military hospitals concerning whom there is so much divergence of opinion, not merely as regards the methods of diagnosis and the mode of treatment that should be adopted, but also with reference to the wider question as to what is to be done with them after their discharge from hospital.

He felt that soldiers suffering from shell-shock ought to be given far more effective treatment in military hospitals throughout Britain, and he deplored the fact that so many of them came under MOs who had no special knowledge of the disorder.[18]

Harold Wiltshire, a physician at a large London hospital, who had spent twelve months attached to military hospitals in France, added his personal views in June, 1916, to the controversy over the causes of

72

shell-shock. He was certain that "the vast majority of cases" arose from an exceptional mental shock, such as the horrible sights on the battlefield, huge losses sustained in an action, or simple fright occasioned by exploding shells, particularly by the fear of being buried when they burst. He did not believe that the condition could originate from wounds, from hardship, or from exposure, and he thought that it was very rarely caused by physical concussion or by the inhalation of noxious gases after a shell had exploded.[19]

Sir Douglas Haig was planning to launch a massive offensive during the early summer of 1916 in the area of the River Somme. He had selected for the operation a fourteen-mile stretch of the Front between Maricourt and Serre. Eighteen Divisions from General Rawlinson's Fourth Army were to take part and the initial assault was to be preceded by the greatest artillery bombardment of the war. Rawlinson informed his corps commanders at a preliminary conference that the five-day barrage would not only destroy all the German barbed wire entanglements but would also pulverize their forward trenches and dugouts, leaving none of their soldiers alive. When the moment came, he said, the British assault troops would merely have to walk across no-man's-land and take possession of the German line. Haig was so obsessed with the magnitude of his forthcoming victory that he recorded in his diary, "I feel that every step in my plan has been taken with Divine help".[20]

After the bombardment had continued for a few days units in the front line were reporting back that the Germans were still operating from their forward trenches and that considerable portions of their wire were still intact. These reports were dismissed by staff officers as being the outcome of cowardly imagination.[21]

At dawn on 1 July 60,000 British troops stood waiting to go "over the top", unaware that the barrage, intended to annihilate the enemy, had been wholly inadequate for the task. A German soldier has recounted what happened next. Their own men were in position and ready, he said, when they saw a series of extended lines of infantry emerging from the British trenches. "The first line appeared to continue without end to right and left," he went on. "It was quickly followed by a second line, then a third and fourth. They came on at a steady pace as if expecting to find nothing alive in our front trenches." The Germans held their fire until the leading waves were well into no-man's-land, then they opened up with all their weapons. He described the carnage which followed:

> Whole sections seemed to fall, and the rear formations, moving in close order, quickly scattered. The advance crumbled under this hail of shells and bullets. All along the line men could be seen throwing up their arms and collapsing, never to move again. Badly wounded rolled about in their agony, and others less severely injured, crawled to the nearest shellhole for shelter.[22]

The attack was kept up until nightfall and at the end of the day the British casualties numbered 57,470 officers and men, of whom more than 19,000 were listed as killed or died of wounds. The official history of the campaign makes the bitter comment that "for this disastrous loss of the finest manhood of the United Kingdom and Ireland" there had only been an advance into the enemy position of about a mile on a three-and-a-half-mile front.[23] A corporal in the Royal Welch Fusiliers protested that no gain of territory could have been worth the terrible price paid by the BEF on the opening day of the Battle of the Somme. "It was sheer bloody murder," he said.[24]

Several days later a corporal in the Rifle Brigade, whose battalion had just moved into the line, looked out across no-man's-land at the aftermath of the battle:

> As far as you could see there were all these bodies lying out there – literally thousands of them, just where they'd been caught on the First of July. Some of them without legs, some legs without bodies, and arms without bodies. A terrible sight![25]

Chapter 11

It might have been expected that the horrifying slaughter of 1 July, 1916, would have resulted in a change of strategy by the British High Command – a realization that the development of the fire-power of modern weaponry had put an end to the concept of frontal attacks by massed infantry battalions. Unfortunately the message did not get through. The senior British military officers were elderly, unimaginative professionals from the old peacetime army, says the historian A.J.P. Taylor, and they refused to contemplate any change in the established pattern of warfare.[1]

The BEF maintained its offensive in the Somme for the whole of the months of July and August, with mounting casualties and no appreciable gains of territory. After eight weeks of protracted fighting, Haig notified the War Cabinet in London that he was satisfied with the results he had so far achieved and he promised to keep up the pressure on the enemy until well into the autumn. The casualties the Germans would sustain, he said, would "amply compensate" for those of the British.[2] It was an awesome example of the sterile military philosophy of a war of attrition.

Naturally the fighting in the Somme was causing a massive increase in the number of reported shell-shock cases, which was said to have risen to such proportions that it had created something of a military crisis.[3] It was easy enough to blame the breakdown in resilience and morale on the quality of the recent recruits, particularly the conscripted men who were now starting to join the units in the field. However, in addition to the suspected shirkers who had not volunteered for service, conscription was taking in youths who had just reached the age of 18 and would have been too young to have joined up before, even if they had wished to do so.

A private in the Wiltshire Regiment, who took part in an attack in the Somme, has described how he was waiting to go "over the top" beside a young recruit, newly arrived in the battalion in a draft from England. The youth was a bundle of nerves, he said, shaking like a leaf. He was unable to fix his bayonet and was scarcely able to hold his rifle.[4]

In the middle of July, 1916, the Commanding-Officer of the 1/5 Royal Warwicks sent a report to his Brigadier complaining about "the large percentage of utterly useless men" in his battalion. Five days previously, he said, they had captured a German trench and had occupied it with a detachment of forty men. It had almost been re-captured by a small enemy bombing party, because a number of his detachment were incapable of using their rifles or their bayonets. "This class of man is petrified with fear when he meets a German in the flesh," he continued. "There are about a hundred of such men in my battalion, and I would prefer to be without them."[5]

The Brigadier forwarded the report to the Divisional Commander, endorsing it with his own opinion that the soldiers in question were "wasters" – physically weak and lacking in fighting spirit. The Divisional Commander, in his turn, submitted the report to the Corps Commander with a recommendation that about a hundred men should be transferred from the 1/5 Royal Warwicks to the labour battalions which were unloading ships at the base. This proposal was acceptable to the Corps Commander, except that he thought it preferable for the men to work as labourers at the Home Ports. "These men are degenerates," he wrote in a minute. "They are a source of danger to their comrades, their battalion, and the brigade."[6]

Apparently there were certain officers, too, who were arousing the indignation of the High Command because of their supposed reluctance to come to grips with the enemy. The following General Order went out in France during the summer of 1916 under the heading "Officers – Fitness For Duty":

Instances have recently come to notice where an officer without any definite manifestations of a physical disability or injury, has asserted his inability to perform military duty, on

76

the ground that he is the subject of defects in health or temperament.

In future, where the assessment of an officer's fitness for duty depends wholly or in part on his own statement, the officer will be required to sign a written statement clearly setting forth the history and present particulars of the condition which brings his capacity, physically or temperamentally, into question.

This statement will be attached to the correspondence when reference is made to higher authority, and reports by a medical officer, or by a Medical Board, will invariably note the absence or presence of any physical sign (and probable date of origin) which bear relation to any points mentioned in the statement, and will include an opinion as to whether the officer is or is not fit for general service, from his own statement.[7]

Whereas Lord Moran had the greatest admiration for the majority of the junior officers in the BEF, he thought that others, who had come in under the shadow of compulsion, were "plainly worthless fellows". He saw one of the latter sitting at the bottom of a forward trench with his head in his hands. He could be no good to the men of 1916, said Moran; "He had none of the extreme signs of fear; he was just a worthless chap, without shame; the worst product of the towns."[8]

It was not only junior officers who broke down in battle; it could happen to senior officers as well if they happened to remain near the front line long enough. On the first day of the Battle of the Somme a Brigadier-General in one of the attacking Divisions established his advance Brigade Headquarters in a deep and well-constructed dugout. The locality had been subjected to heavy and constant shelling by the Germans. In the evening a sergeant, who had been instructed by the Brigade Major to escort the Brigadier back to the rear, found him slumped in a chair, staring at a hanging lamp like a man in a dream. "He was broken", said the sergeant. "He made no objection to coming with me. He just got up very, very slowly and during a break in the shelling we went out."[9]

The records of courts of enquiry in the Army are rarely to be found in military archives. There is, however, still extant, a transcript of the evidence taken at an interesting Court of Enquiry into "The failure of a party of the 11th Border Regiment to carry out an attack on 10 July, 1916".[10]

The 11th Borders had been one of the assault battalions in the catastrophic offensive on 1 July. During that day they had lost all their officers and over 500 of their men. About 250 of the survivors had been left in the front line under the command of a Captain Palmer, who belonged to another regiment. On 9 July Palmer had been ordered by his Brigadier to send out a party that night, consisting of two officers and 100 other ranks, with the object of capturing a portion of the enemy's front trench and attacking his support line. Palmer detailed 2nd Lieutenant Ross and 2nd Lieutenant Twynham to lead the raid and, because of the numerical weakness of the battalion, had instructed them to find their other ranks from the reserves behind the line. In fact only ninety men were available.

It had been arranged that the party would set off into no-man's-land just after midnight, but at about half past nine that evening Ross reported to Palmer that about a third of the men who had been selected for the raid had applied to see the MO, complaining that they were suffering from shell-shock and insisting that their nerves were too bad for them to take part. At first Palmer forbade the men to report sick and ordered that they should go on the raid. However, when they continued to claim that it would be impossible to comply with his order because of the state of their nerves, he arranged for the MO, Lieutenant Kirkwood, to examine them and to decide whether or not they were fit for duty. At eleven o'clock that evening Kirkwood held an impromptu sick parade. Having examined each of the men in turn, he signed a certificate in which he stated:

> In view of the bombing raid to be carried out by the 11th Border Regiment, I must hereby testify to their unfitness for such an operation as few, if any, are not suffering from some degree of shell-shock.

Lieutenant Kirkwood told the Court of Enquiry that he had formed his opinion because he realized that what had happened to the battalion on 1 July had had a most demoralizing effect on these men and they had not yet had time to recover their equilibrium. They had

78

spent the time ever since carrying up rations to the front line under heavy shellfire, sorting out the kits of their dead comrades, burying the dead in trenches and living in an atmosphere of decomposing corpses. In addition, they had been kept in open trenches under continuous shellfire and had had little opportunity for sleep.

Just before midnight on the evening of the raid Palmer had sent Ross back to Brigade Headquarters with the MO's certificate. The Brigadier had decided to ignore it and had ordered that the operation should proceed according to plan.

Ross and Twynham assembled their reluctant party and told them to draw grenades from the weapon store, but some of men declined to do so. They then began to move forward along the communication trench towards the front line, with Ross in the lead and Twynham bringing up the rear. Progress was very slow because some of the men lagged behind and others kept taking wrong turnings. After an hour of this they had only covered half the distance to the point where they would leave the trench and start crossing no-man's-land. Ross had realized, as he said later, that there was "a great lack of offensive spirit in the party" and that there was no possibility of their keeping to the prescribed time schedule, so, on his own initiative, he cancelled the operation.

When Palmer informed Brigade Headquarters what had happened the Brigadier immediately ordered that the four sergeants in the party should be placed under arrest for "failing in their duty". The Court of Enquiry was set up soon afterwards to establish the exact reason why the raid had not taken place.

Before the Brigadier submitted the transcript of the evidence taken before the Enquiry to his Divisional Commander, he added his own observations to the document. He said that, despite the fact that all the officers in the 11th Borders had become casualties within the first half-hour of the attack on 1 July, he had had no idea, and nobody had told him, that the battalion was in such a state of demoralization. He had believed them to be in good spirits. Many other units, in his opinion, would not have "collapsed" as this battalion had done. He went on to dispute Lieutenant Kirkwood's evidence that twenty men had been sent back from the 11th Borders suffering from shell-shock on the day the raid had been ordered. As far as he knew there had been practically no cases of shell-shock within his entire brigade.

The Divisional Commander also added a note of his own views on the matter before he sent on the papers to his superiors. In a mild reproof to the Brigadier he said that he thought it was a pity that the 11th Borders had been detailed for this operation under the prevailing circumstances, as the battalion had done excellent work since they had joined the BEF. With regard to the four arrested sergeants, the Judge Advocate's Department had informed him that there was no evidence to support charges against any of them. He himself had no doubt whatsoever as to who was really responsible for the debacle. "The MO was to blame," he asserted, "and he has been relieved."

The papers reached the Army Commander, General Sir Hubert Gough, on 17 July and he reacted in his customary forthright and impulsive way. Without delay, he drafted a memorandum, in which he stated:

> It is inconceivable how men, who have pledged themselves to fight and uphold the honour of their country, could degrade themselves in such a manner, and show an utter want of manly spirit and courage which, at least, is expected of every soldier and Britisher. The conduct on the part of Lieutenant Kirkwood RAMC shows him to be totally unfitted to hold a commission in the Army, or to exercise any military responsibility. Immediate steps must be taken to remove Lieutenant Kirkwood from the service.

The next day the Assistant Director of Medical Services in the Division to which the 11th Border Regiment was attached, wrote to General Gough asking to reconsider his decision regarding Lieutenant Kirkwood's dismissal from the Army. Kirkwood, he said, had been the MO in this battalion since October, 1915, and had performed his duties conscientiously and well. The sick rate in his battalion had never been excessive and he had done very good work in attending to the wounded during the recent fighting. The late Commanding Officer of the 11th Borders had had a high opinion of him. The ADMS's plea fell on deaf ears. General Gough had made up his mind and he was adamant that Kirkwood must go.

The final Minute in the file dealing with this episode was written at the end of July, 1916, by Surgeon-General Sir Arthur Sloggett, the Director-General of Medical Services at the time. He pointed out that Kirkwood had been asked to give his opinion; he did so, and it was disregarded. He concluded, "The whole case is deplorable. The MO appears to have been made the scapegoat."

It was estimated that during the twelve-month period before 30 April, 1916, a total of approximately 1,300 officers and 10,000 other ranks had been admitted to the special hospitals in Britain for shell-shock patients. In addition, an increasing number of cases were being treated in France without being sent home.[11]

Throughout the early stages of the Battle of the Somme Dr Charles S. Myers had remained as the War Office Consultant Neurologist to the BEF, but in August, 1916, his designation was altered to "Consultant Psychologist". By then some of the British Army bases in France had their own mental wards for shell-shock patients and these were gradually being staffed by specialists in mental illness. A further development had been the setting-up of several advanced neurological centres in forward areas, where soldiers suffering from milder forms of shell-shock could be treated and then returned to the Front. Most of the shell-shocked men who were evacuated to the bases were sent back to England as soon as possible. In July, 1916, a General Order was issued that any patient in a mental ward at a base who was, in the opinion of the Medical Officer in charge, affected by nervous exhaustion "arising from insufficient self-control" and who was likely to recover in a short time should, whenever possible, be kept in France for treatment.[12]

At this time Charles Myers wanted to write a book about shell-shock based upon his recent experience with over 2,000 shell-shocked patients. However, the military authorities still regarded the subject as being highly sensitive and he was told by the Director-General of Medical Services that the General Staff were "strongly opposed" even to articles being written about it.[13] In fact, Myers' book was not published until long after the war.

In common with a number of other doctors who were obtaining firsthand knowledge of shell-shock, Myers had reached the conclusion that the condition could result either from the effects of bursting shells, or from excessive strain, caused, for instance, by long-continued fear, horror, anxiety, exposure or fatigue. He thought that insomnia was a predisposing factor.[14]

Myers' views on the origins of shell-shock were shared by Dr William Brown, a specialist in psychological medicine, who at that time was in charge of one of the advanced neurological centres in France, and was later to become Commandant of Craiglockhart, the well-known wartime hospital in Scotland for officers with war neurosis. At the neurological centre Dr Brown saw most of the shell-shocked men within forty-eight hours from the moment when they had broken down and he had found that hysterical symptoms, such as mutism and paralysis, could often occur after an interval, which might last for several days. In an article he wrote for a medical journal he gave an example of this happening to an officer who had been under heavy shellfire in an outpost and had come to the centre "some days" afterwards suffering from hysterical spasmodic contractions of the abdominal and leg muscles and profuse sweating. The officer told him:

My feelings during the shelling are hard to define, as I was too fully occupied to allow for much thought on the subject. Owing to the small area to which we were confined, there was no opportunity of being able to give vent to the pent-up feelings that were in me, and in consequence my nerves were strung up to such a pitch that I felt that something in me would snap. Every shell seemed to be nearer the mark than the last, and the ground all around was covered with shellholes. The general feeling was that "the next one" would land right in the post. Part of the trench had already been blown in. The back blast from each explosion flattened us up against the wall of the trench.

The days following I was always thinking of this episode, and [at night] I could never sleep, but would just doze and then wake up with a start, with my heart palpitating furiously, and with great difficulty in breathing. I would also find myself in a profuse cold sweat, especially of the scalp, forehead and hands. Then my legs began to be affected and would shake as though I had the ague. This would come on in the day at times, but invariably happened at night when I was lying down.[15]

82

A few days later, said the officer, he had had trouble with his stomach. He felt that something was pulling him forward and his whole body was shaking. These spasms kept on recurring every few minutes. There was a "belt of pain" around his body and the cold sweats continued throughout.[16] Dr Brown did not reveal in his article what had become of this officer after his admission to the neurological centre.

There was a general policy among British, French, and German doctors who were treating soldiers suffering from war neuroses to rid them of their hysterical manifestations as quickly as possible so that they could be returned to the line. Shortage of manpower was then a pressing problem for all three nations. There were some medical officers, however, who doubted the wisdom of such a procedure. Dr Gupp, a German psychiatrist, admitted that he had thought originally that it was his patriotic duty to get his neurotic patients back to the battlefield, but he had soon lost confidence in his ability to do this effectively. Frequently they had further breakdowns, he said, "because under the stress of war, we cannot always expect that those in military command will handle the intensely disturbed soldier with the insight and understanding and the patience of the expert psychiatrist."[17] Professor Julian M. Wolfsohn, of Leland Stanford University, California, agreed with Gupp's opinion, maintaining that, once a patient had suffered from a severe neurosis, his nervous system became more fragile than before and any subsequent "shock" might bring about a serious relapse, with a return of all his previous symptoms.[18]

Senior officers in the BEF continued to regard war neurosis with a mixture of suspicion and contempt, and at a court martial for cowardice or desertion the fact that the accused man had recently undergone treatment for shell-shock was rarely considered to be a mitigating circumstance.

Private Harry Farr of the 1st Battalion, the West Yorkshire Regiment had been in France since November, 1914. Early in May, 1916, he had been sent back to the base suffering from shell-shock. He re-joined the battalion after a few weeks and the following July he was away again for a short time with nervous trouble. On 17 September, 1916, when the 1st West Yorkshires were in the line, a sergeant found Farr in the battalion transport area. He was ordered to return to the trenches, but he refused to do so, saying that he was unfit and could not stand it. Even after the sergeant had detailed a corporal and an escort to take him back to the line, Farr declined to accompany them and when they tried to drag him along he struggled so much that they could not move him. Farr was court-martialled for cowardice on 10 October.[19] A lieutenant who gave evidence at the trial verified that on several occasions Farr had applied to be excused from working-parties at the Front, on the ground that he could not stand shellfire. At the time, he added, Farr had been trembling "and did not appear to be in a fit state". Farr was convicted and sentenced to death. His Commanding Officer endorsed the court-martial papers with the following comment:

> I cannot say what has destroyed this man's nerves, but he had proved himself on many occasions incapable of keeping his head in action and likely to cause a panic. Apart from his behaviour under fire his conduct and character are very good.

No medical evidence was given at Farr's trial and he was not ordered to appear before a Medical Board after his conviction. He was shot at dawn on 18 October, 1916.

2nd Lieutenant Eric Poole, the first officer in the BEF to be executed in pursuance of a court-martial sentence, had also been returned to the line after suffering from shell-shock. He had been posted to the 11th Battalion, the West Yorkshire Regiment in May, 1916, as a newly-commissioned officer. Two months later, during the Battle of the Somme, he was knocked unconscious by a clod of earth displaced by an exploding German shell and had been evacuated to the base with shell-shock. He spent a month in hospital undergoing treatment, and on his discharge he was graded as unfit for service at the Front because of the continuance of his neurotic symptoms. However, this grading was reversed by a Medical Board which decided that he had fully recovered and was fit enough for active service. He had re-joined his battalion, which was then in reserve, but which had gone back into the line in the middle of September. Poole had carried on with his duties until 5 October when he had let it be known that he was feeling unwell. He then disappeared and he had been missing until he was apprehended by the Military Police two days later.

Soon after Poole's arrest his Brigadier had sent a note to the

Divisional commander suggesting that he should be sent home rather than being court-martialled for desertion, in view of the fact that he had just recovered from shell-shock. In spite of this, the court martial went ahead on 21 November, 1916, and Poole was convicted and sentenced to death.[20] There were two pieces of evidence at the trial which might have been expected to tell in his favour. Firstly, the Military Policeman who had arrested him had formed the impression that he was "in a confused state of mind"; and secondly, the Medical Officer of the battalion had expressed his opinion that Poole's return to battle conditions "might well" have caused him to relapse.

Dr Gupp had no doubt that certain men who had broken down in battle would suffer a recurrence of their trouble if they were sent back to the Front, because, he said, their nervous systems were "positively unfitted for the hardships and horrors of war".[21]

Chapter 12

The *Official History of the British Medical Services during the First World War*, which was published in 1923, explained why the Somme battles of 1916 provided "ideal conditions" for the development of war neurosis:

> The "artillery preparation" of the attacking force called for an "artillery reply" from the opposing side. This duel frequently lasted for several hours or days, and during this period of waiting the nerves of all were kept on edge. Then, after the attack came the reckoning of losses amongst comrades; and it was not unlikely that, owing to the call for troops, the whole acute process might soon be repeated. Little by little men became worn down by such experience, and despite their best efforts that the time would come when it was impossible to keep their thoughts from preying on the ordeals and sights of the battlefield. In such instances a breakdown occurred slowly; a gradual change would be noticed in the demeanour and behaviour of the patient, and he would eventually reach hospital with the report that he was "quite useless in the line". Another large group consisted of those cases in which a man suffering from an incipient "breakdown", or even to all appearances perfectly well, was suddenly faced with an experience of inexpressible horror which completely broke down his self-control.[1]

From July, 1916, onwards there had been a great influx of soldiers with nervous disorders into hospitals in England. By then, the *Official*

History continues, the term "shell-shock" had become a generally recognized classification, as if it were an unknown disease, whereas exactly similar cases had been familiar to doctors before the war.

> Indeed, certain members of the profession lectured and wrote on the subject as if it were some new and mysterious malady. A complex terminology was evolved, and special treatments were manufactured in bewildering profusion . . . which could not fail to impress on the soldier's mind the mysteriousness of his malady.[2]

During the latter months of 1916 the attitude of the military authorities in the BEF towards shell-shock underwent a marked change. For one thing, they finally accepted that it was a genuine disorder, the origins of which were psychological.[3] For another, they realized that the severe wastage of manpower it was causing on the Western Front was accentuated by the lack of proper medical organization to deal with this particular type of illness soon after it occurred. Nevertheless, it was considered, in the interests of army discipline, that when a soldier in the line suffered a nervous breakdown, his condition should be carefully investigated in the battle area and he should only be evacuated to the base where such a course was absolutely necessary.[4]

It was proposed by Lieut-Colonel Myers and Lieut-Colonel Holmes, respectively the Consulting Psychologist and the Consulting Neurologist to the BEF, that there should be a special centre in each army area for the diagnosis and treatment of psychoneurosis cases. The recommendation was adopted and four centres were opened in the autumn of 1916. A fifth was added the following summer. The Adjutant-General had issued an order that every patient who "without any visible wound becomes non-effective from the effects of British or enemy weapons in action" must be sent to a special centre for examination. While he was there his Commanding Officer had to provide a full report on the circumstances under which he had become a casualty. It was then decided whether the patient would be classified as "wounded" or as "sick".[5]

The military authorities were still anxious to segregate the soldiers who were suffering from authentic psychoneurosis from those who were afflicted with what was regarded as "insufficient stoutness of heart". During periods of violent fighting approximately 50 per cent of the cases admitted to the special centres were graded as "wounded" and 50 per cent as "sick". In times of comparative quiescence about 40 per cent were classed as "wounded" and about 60 per cent as "sick". Whenever possible, patients remained at the centres for treatment until they could be returned to their units. Any cases which were sent down the line had to be evacuated to a special neurological hospital at the base.[6]

Around this time a greater awareness of the true nature of war neurosis was becoming apparent in the military hospitals in Britain. An army neurologist, Dr Ballard, wrote in an article that physicians who had been dealing extensively with shell-shock patients had developed new ideas about the disorder and, at the same time, had been satisfied that some old theories were correct. In his opinion, blowing up by a shell, or burial as a result of its explosion, was not the primary cause so much as the "last straw" in the production of psychoneurosis. Soldiers were human beings with human instincts, he said. When they came under fire, especially shellfire, they were afraid. The instinct of self-preservation became paramount and their involuntary reaction was to run away. Counterbalancing this was the sense of duty to remain. A struggle took place in their minds and normally their fear was suppressed, but if they continued in action it might re-emerge, perhaps as the result of an incident like seeing a friend wounded or perhaps without any incident at all, and they could develop neurasthenic symptoms.[7]

At the close of the year 1916 the fortunes of the Allies were at a low ebb. The Somme offensive and the Gallipoli campaign had been costly failures. The French had almost exhausted all their available reserves of manpower and the Russian Army was fast disintegrating.

The total strength of the BEF was then about 1,200,000 officers and men; the losses in the Somme battles had amounted to more than 420,000 killed, wounded, or missing. Sir Douglas Haig had been promised nine new divisions by the spring of 1917 and he had informed the War Cabinet and the French High Command that he would be ready to resume the offensive in February.

On the Western Front the winter of 1916-1917 was wet and bleak. The rain poured down ceaselessly, adding to the misery of the troops in the trenches and churning the earth into a waterlogged morass. One of Haig's Corps Commanders warned him that "No one who has not visited the Front can really know the state of exhaustion to which our men are reduced".[8] Conscription was yielding a steady stream of recruits to the battalions in the line, but they were not always of the quality of the volunteers of the past. Siegfried Sassoon, an experienced and decorated infantry officer, wrote:

> The raw material to be trained was growing steadily worse. Most of those who came in now had joined the Army unwillingly and there was no reason why they should find military service tolerable. The war had become undisguisedly mechanical and inhuman. What in earlier days had been drafts of volunteers were now droves of victims.[9]

In the middle of January, 1917, intermittent frosts had started to harden the ground in front of the British line and Haig carried out a series of limited attacks, some of which were moderately successful. However, he had decided to postpone his main offensive until April when his own and French forces under General Nivelle would launch a joint attack. Meanwhile the German High Command had decided to withdraw from their trenches on the Somme to new positions between Lens and Rheims.

At the end of January 1917 Germany informed the United States of America that she was about to begin an unrestricted submarine campaign against the merchant shipping of neutral nations. Throughout the months of February and March, and during the first week of April, American vessels were sunk by U-boat action, and American lives were lost. Finally, on 6 April, the United States entered the war on the side of the allies and pledged the use of all her resources to bring the conflict to a successful termination. Winston Churchill has observed that "Of all the grand miscalculations of the German High Command none is more remarkable than their inability to comprehend the meaning of war with the American Union."[10]

An American Expeditionary Force was prepared immediately to fight alongside the British and French troops on the Western Front. General Pershing, who was to be its Commander-in-Chief, aimed at having a million men in the field by 1918 and three million a year later.

The attitude of the American Army with regard to war neurosis was both sensible and realistic. It was arranged that Dr Thomas W. Salmon, a Major in the Medical Officers' Reserve Corps and Medical Director of the National Committee for Mental Hygiene, should visit English military hospitals to study the subject, and on his return to America should report his conclusions to the Surgeon-General. Dr Salmon explained the object of his assignment:

> No medico-military problems of the war are more striking than those growing out of the extraordinary incidence of mental and functional nervous diseases ("shell-shock"). Together these disorders are responsible for not less than one-seventh of all discharges for disability from the British Army, or one-third if discharges from wounds are excluded. A medical service newly confronted like ours with the task of caring for the sick and wounded of a large army cannot ignore such important causes of invalidism. . . . My visit to England was for the purpose of observing these matters at first hand so that I could contribute information which might help for dealing with mental and nervous diseases among our own forces when they are exposed to the terrific stress of modern warfare.[11]

Another American doctor who came over to England at much the same time as Dr Salmon for the purpose of studying shell-shock was Dr John T. MacCurdy of the New York Psychiatric Institute. He visited Moss Side Hospital at Maghull, eighteen miles from Liverpool, and Craiglockhart Officers' Hospital in Scotland. On his return to America he gave a series of lectures to psychiatrists and neurologists who would be coming to Europe with the American Expeditionary Force.

Dr Salmon learned that about 6,000 men from the BEF were being admitted annually to military hospitals in England as insane. In his opinion, even in 1917, it was by no means rare for a soldier with shell-shock to be mistakenly categorized as being insane, or for an insane soldier to be thought to have shell-shock. He said that twenty-one asylums or similar institutions in Great Britain and Ireland had been converted into military hospitals and there was a suspicion among the public that soldiers with mental diseases were being sent to them as "pauper lunatics". He added that in England insanity and pauperism had always been closely associated.[12]

In his report to the Surgeon-General, Dr Salmon discussed the argument that shell-shock patients required so much care and so few recoveries were achieved that it would be preferable to send home every American soldier who was afflicted with the disorder. He thought that such a procedure would be unfortunate from a military and from a humanitarian standpoint. One of its immediate effects would be to increase the prevalence of shell-shock in the AEF. "In the unending conflict between duty, honour and discipline, on the one hand," he said, "and homesickness, horror and the urgings of the instinct of self-preservation, on the other, war neurosis – as a way out – is already accessible enough to most men without calling attention to it by the adoption of such an administrative policy." In his opinion, if it was known in the Army that anyone suffering from shell-shock would automatically be returned home and discharged, it would be all too easy for a soldier to simulate the disorder.[13]

Dr Salmon put forward three urgent recommendations for the AEF. Firstly, the importance of providing, in advance, adequate facilities for the treatment of nervous and mental disorders "could hardly be overstated"; secondly, care must be taken to prevent the insane, the feeble-minded and the neuropaths from enlisting in the Army; and thirdly, a careful watch must be kept on troops during their training to observe if any of them developed psychopathic tendencies.

He thought that it was highly desirable to make use of all available information about the nature of shell-shock and he went on:

> The lesson to be learnt from the British results seems clear – that treatment by medical officers with special training in psychiatry should be made available just as near the front as military exigency will permit, and that patients who cannot be reached at this point should be treated at special hospitals in France until it is apparent that they cannot be returned to the firing line.

Any soldier who was going to be permanently unfit for further duty, he said, should be sent home as soon as possible.[14]

Dr Salmon's suggestions were immediately accepted and put into effect by the authorities. A Neurology and Psychiatry Branch was set up in the office of the Surgeon-General and it was decided that a medical officer with special training in mental and nervous disorders would be allocated to every combat division in the AEF. Salmon had emphasized the necessity for the early treatment of shell-shock cases, so small units were organized in advanced positions on the Western Front for the observation and care of war neurosis patients, in addition to regular neuropsychiatric hospitals at all the American Army bases. As there were insufficient qualified psychiatrists available to meet the vast requirements of the military, intensive six-week courses were arranged to teach medical officers how to recognize and how to treat shell-shock casualties in the forward battle areas.[15]

The Head of the Neurology and Psychiatry Branch of the Surgeon-General's office visited American military hospitals in France during the summer of 1917 soon after the AEF had first been in action. On his return he reported that, unless special measures were taken, there was every indication that American soldiers would develop neuroses to a degree even greater than had occurred among the British. The conditions of American life, he said, were such that a young man nearly always had his own way, obedience was never required from him and he had been taught that he was the equal of everyone else. The troops in the AEF were taken suddenly from that environment, to be transposed into a system of rigid discipline and brought face to face with all the horrors or war. It would not be surprising, he observed, if they reacted to the change by developing neuroses. French neurologists had told him of the excessive nervousness of American soldiers who had been under their care.[16]

The increasing awareness of the true nature of war neurosis among the higher officers in the BEF does not appear to have resulted in the more humane treatment of the mentally disordered soldiers who were charged with cowardice or desertion. The only court-martial files still extant are those in which the accused men were executed. The opinions of the senior commanders as to whether or not a death sentence should be carried out clearly indicate the lack of sympathy they felt for the soldiers who broke down.

A 19-year-old private in the Hampshire Regiment went absent from the front line in August, 1916. At his trial on a charge of cowardice it came out that he had been to hospital several times suffering from nervous complaints and his Company Sergeant-Major had said in evidence that "as soon as shelling starts, he goes all to pieces and goes practically off his head through sheer terror". In spite of the Commanding Officer's opinion that the man had not known what he was doing when he left the trenches, his Corps Commander wrote on the papers:

> Cowards of this sort are a serious danger to the army. The death penalty is instituted to make such men fear running away more than they fear the enemy.[17]

A private in a Scottish regiment was court-martialled for desertion a week later. He had gone absent while his battalion was under heavy fire from gas shells and he claimed that he had lost his memory. The battalion Medical Officer was called as a defence witness. He verified that the man's nerves were in a bad condition at the time and that "he seemed to be suffering from the strain of events". All the senior commanders recommended that the death penalty should be enforced, except one who made no comment.[18]

A 20-year-old lance-corporal in the Cheshire Regiment had been standing in a front-line trench when a shell had exploded nearby and the brains of the man beside him were spattered across his face. After this incident he was continually going sick with shell-shock and eventually he deserted. Before he was convicted at his trial in November, 1916, the Court called his Medical Officer, but he was unable to give any evidence about the corporal's mental condition. The senior officers did not consider it necessary to obtain a proper medical report before the death sentence was confirmed.[19]

Two deserters who were court-martialled and shot just before the end of 1916 both had their Commanding Officers standing up for them, to no avail. In the first case the Colonel had said the accused man's nerves were so bad that any shelling made him tremble with fear.[20] In the second, the Colonel had described how the deserter had panicked whenever he came under fire and had seemed to be "quite incapable of self-control".[21]

Even in 1917 the official attitude in the BEF remained uncompromising with regard to soldiers whose nerves were shattered by the terrors in the battlefield. At the trial of a deserter who was executed in June of that year the Court was told that soon after going absent from the line he had appeared dazed and was unable to give a satisfactory account of himself.[22] Another deserter, tried two weeks later, said in evidence that since being wounded earlier in the war he had never been the same man again and had been terrified of shellfire. This did not save him from being shot at dawn.[23]

Chapter 13

On 9 April, 1917, three days after the United States of America had entered the war, Haig launched his spring offensive in the neighbourhood of Arras. At first light thousands of British and Canadian troops crouched shoulder to shoulder in front line trenches, deep in slush and mud, waiting to go over the top. The weather was appalling for that time of year – bitterly cold, with squalls of rain, sleet, and even snow. For the past forty-eight hours the artillery had been pounding the German positions with 2879 guns.

Just before the attack had started NCOs had gone round, as always, to give each man a tot of extremely alcoholic Navy rum. The teetotallers usually gave away their share, and the previous year, on the Somme, two soldiers had consumed so much rum that they had passed out in the bottom of the trench. There had been another incident in a different regiment, when confusion had arisen at the moment of the assault because the whole of the leading wave was so drunk.[1]

At 5.30 that morning, in obedience to whistle-blasts and shouted commands, the men started to clamber over the parapet and to advance across no-man's-land through a lethal hail of bullets with their bayonets at the ready. Behind them the stretcher-bearers were busy picking up the wounded and rushing them back to the Regimental Aid Post. The attack was successful. Almost the whole of the German first-line trench system was overrun and the Canadians captured the dominating plateau of Vimy Ridge. During the next few days the German resistance had stiffened and any further territorial gains were only achieved at considerable cost.

In the middle of April the French forces under General Nivelle had launched their own great offensive in the southern part of the line. They made little progress and sustained enormous losses. By the beginning of May the nature of the fighting on the whole of the Western Front had once again become static.

In a report to the War Cabinet in London, Haig wrote:

> The enemy's fighting strength is not yet broken, and it is essential to realize that it can only be broken by hard and continual fighting . . . The first step must always be to wear down ("soften", as it is said nowadays) the enemy's power of resistance until he is so weakened that he will not be able to withstand a decisive blow.[2]

The "softening-up" process during the previous few weeks had accounted for more than 80,000 British casualties.

In February, 1917, General Headquarters in France had issued instructions that soldiers who had been shell-shocked as a result of their proximity to exploding shells should continue to be categorized as "shell-shock wounded". If they had recovered after treatment at a Special Centre or a Base Hospital they were to be posted back to their units and kept on regimental fatigues for one month before being returned to full duty in the line.[3]

There was still a great deal of suspicion among the senior officers on the General Staff that a high proportion of the men reporting sick with shell-shock were malingerers. For this reason, in June, 1917, the Adjutant-General issued an order to all the Special Centres in France that on the admission of every new patient a form would be completed describing his condition and the supposed cause of his disorder. This would then be sent to his Commanding Officer who would have to state whether or not the soldier had been "subjected to exceptional exposure" before he had broken down. The patient's medical documents were to be marked "NYDN" (Not Yet Diagnosed, Nervous) until his Commanding Officer's reply had been received and it had been decided if he should be graded as "Shell-Shock Wounded" or as "Shell-Shock Sick".[4]

There had been considerable doubt at an earlier stage of the war as to whether or not a soldier who had been discharged from the Army because he was suffering from shell-shock would be entitled to receive a disability pension. In July, 1917, the Minister of Pensions, replying to a question in the House of Commons, said that, in view of the special difficulties involved with discharged neurasthenic and shell-shocked soldiers, a Special Medical Board had been established to deal with all such cases and had been empowered to grant them pensions or gratuities. Branch medical boards had been set up in Scotland and Ireland to perform a similar function. Provision was being made for men who had already been discharged with neurasthenia or shell-shock before the new system was introduced to be re-examined. The Minister assured the House that every man who was invalided from the forces because he had shell-shock would be awarded a pension, or if he was less seriously affected, a gratuity. In addition, he would be eligible for free treatment and resettlement training. Several hospitals were being provided for this purpose and other patients were being sent to recuperate on farms in Essex.[5]

Answering a further question a few weeks later, the Minister of Pensions said that the Special Medical Board consisted of fifty members. They sat every day in London and visited some town in the provinces once every three weeks. The Board had the right to refuse to discharge a soldier when it was proper to do so, but they used this power very sparingly. So far they had considered 5,000 cases and they had only refused a discharge in fifty of them.[6]

The French Army mutinies started at the end of April and worsened during May. They were mainly brought about by the war-weariness of the troops, their huge losses and their lack of confidence in their leaders. Discontent had also been fomented by the subversive literature which was circulating among them. The result was a complete breakdown of discipline. Entire regiments marched on Paris to demand a negotiated peace settlement with Germany; there were instances of units refusing to serve on the line, of officers being threatened or assaulted, and acts of sabotage being committed on stores and equipment at various bases. Mass desertions were reported and fifty-five men were executed by firing squads for offences of ill-discipline. On 15 May General Nivelle was dismissed and General Pétain became the Commander-in-Chief of the French Army. Pétain immediately set about the restoration of the Army's shattered morale, but it was obvious that he was faced with a lengthy task and that for months ahead the French forces on the Western Front would not be ready to participate in any new offensive.

Haig accepted the fact that for the time being the BEF would have to bear the brunt of the battle, but nevertheless he remained confident of his ability to beat the Germans decisively before the end of 1917. He informed the War Cabinet in June of his conviction that "if the fighting was kept up at its present intensity for six months Germany would be at the end of her available manpower". For this reason he had planned to launch another offensive in Flanders later in the summer.[7]

While the new attack was still in preparation Tank Corps Headquarters in Belgium submitted a disquieting memorandum to the General Staff. They gave a warning that the area over which the troops would have to advance was subject to intensive flooding and had always been considered too wet for cultivation. If the existing drainage was destroyed by bombardment, they said, the whole battlefield would be turned into a vast swamp.[8] In the event, their advice was ignored.

In June, 1917, Lieut-Colonel Charles Myers, the Consulting Psychologist to the BEF, examined the French Army's methods of dealing with soldiers suffering from war neurosis. All French shell-shock patients, except those who had been wounded, were segregated from other casualties at the forward sorting hospitals and were sent immediately to one of the Army Neurological Centres. These were situated about fifteen miles behind the front line and it was estimated that most of the patients were admitted to them within eight hours from the onset of their symptoms. The British Advanced Neurological Centres were further from the Front and soldiers who had broken down in battle took much longer to reach them.[9]

A large number of shell-shock casualties in the BEF were transferred to Base Hospitals and a considerable proportion were still being sent back to Britain. The French Neurological Centres evacuated very few of their patients to hospitals at the rear, but attempted, whenever possible, to keep them under treatment until they were fit enough for duty. They were then given seven days' leave before returning to the line. The doctors believed that the prospect of a period of leave provided an incentive for the soldiers to recover.[10]

98

The French Neurological Centre visited by Myers had 200 beds. There was no nursing sister, he said, "and a somewhat dreary atmosphere prevailed". He thought that too many patients were being kept in complete isolation. He was also critical of the excessive use of electric shocks for treating hysteria, mutism, paralysis and other neurotic disorders. This had led to parliamentary protests in Paris and allegations that shell-shocked soldiers were being subjected to torture. Myers doubted whether such a perfunctory system as that which was evident in this Neurological Centre would be capable of bringing about many permanent cures and he considered the régime too strict and too harsh for the more serious cases. On the other hand, he thought that the British methods for treating shell-shock at that time should have been more purposeful, and he was opposed to keeping the milder cases in such comfortable and pleasant conditions that it tended to make them reluctant to recover quickly.[11]

Each of the French Armies had its own Psychiatric Centre in a rear area for the treatment of the more severe cases which had been sent back by the Neurological Centres. They also received soldiers diagnosed as insane. Their principal aim was to restore the neurotic men to fitness for full duty.[12] Professor Léri, who worked at the Psychiatric Centre of the 2nd French Army, claimed that from July to October, 1916, 91 percent of their patients had been returned to the fighting line.[13]

As a result of his study of the French system, Myers proposed to the Director-General of Medical Services that a Forward Sorting Centre with accommodation for 250 shell-shock patients should be established by each of the Armies in the BEF. Only one Army actually adopted this suggestion and their Forward Sorting Centre was soon closed on the directions of General Headquarters, which disapproved of the scheme.[14]

The BEF began another offensive on 7 June, 1917. During the next week, at a cost of about 24,000 casualties, they penetrated the German defences to a depth of between one and two miles and captured the entire high ground of the Messines Ridge.

Haig was determined to give the enemy no respite and to attack in the immediate future across the Flanders plains. The area he selected was a vast reclaimed marshland in which the soggy ground was subject to constant flooding. The assault was to open on the last day of July.

It was preceded by a ten-day bombardment which had the effect of destroying most of the dykes and converting the earth into a quagmire. Ten infantry divisions took part in the first day of the offensive, attacking on an eleven-mile front. They lost over 31,000 men and made an advance of about 3,000 yards. Thus began what was officially styled the "Third Battle of Ypres" but it is more often remembered by the name of the town where some of the bitterest fighting took place – Passchendaele. It was not a battle so much as a campaign, said Liddell Hart, and it was "so fruitless in its results, so depressing in its direction" that it has become "a synonym for military failure – a name black-bordered in the records of the British Army".[15]

At the close of the first day General Gough, whose Army had been involved in the hardest fighting and had suffered the most severe casualties, advised that the operations should be discontinued. Haig did not agree. He reported to the War Cabinet that the initial results of the attack had been "highly satisfactory" and that the losses had been "slight for such a great battle".[16] After the offensive had continued for a month without making any real progress Lloyd George, now the British Prime Minister, suggested to Haig that he should husband his declining resources of manpower until the French and American Armies would be in a position to lend him more positive support, but Haig remained supremely confident that if he persisted a short while longer the German forces in Flanders would be totally defeated.

By the early autumn the battlefield had deteriorated into a vast wilderness of liquid mud, with scarcely a tree, a hedge or a building left standing. Ammunition and supplies had to be carried forward to the trenches along narrow duckboard tracks, which formed the only access through the swamps on either side. The evacuation of the wounded was difficult, slow, and agonizing under such circumstances.

Eventually, early in November, Haig's troops entered the deserted, wrecked and tactically valueless town of Passchendaele. It was the end of a campaign which had brought the BEF to the verge of exhaustion and in which they had suffered 238,000 casualties.[17]

Out of all the British soldiers who broke down in action during Haig's Passchendaele offensive, the official figures show that a total of 267 officers and 3,771 other ranks were listed as "battle casualties" due to shell-shock.[18] The tables do not record the numbers graded as "shell-shock sick", neither could they reveal how many men who did not report sick were suffering from neurotic disorders.

At this stage of the war the British public had become well aware of the "mysterious illness" known as "shell-shock" and a small group of Labour MPs were becoming increasingly concerned about shell-shocked soldiers being executed for military offences committed in the front line. In October, 1917, the Under-Secretary of State for War assured the House of Commons that death sentences were only passed at courts martial "after the most careful and thorough investigations" had been made.[19] Philip Snowden, the leader of the Independent Labour Party, had then pressed him about the case of a 21-year-old private in the Royal Scots Fusiliers, executed for desertion the previous August, who had been treated for shell-shock and returned to the Front "completely nerve-shattered". The Under-Secretary stated in reply that he was not prepared to interfere with the discretion of General Haig, the Commander-in-Chief, who had confirmed the death sentence after giving his fullest consideration to the facts.[20] The soldier in question had been detained in a lunatic asylum in Scotland while he was a teenager. He had become a Special Reservist before the war and had joined the BEF in September, 1914. The following month he was injured when his dugout had been blown up by a shell and he was evacuated to England suffering from shell-shock. It is not clear from the papers when he returned to France. At any rate, he was back with his battalion in July, 1917, when he had deserted a few days before the opening of the Passchendaele offensive. He had offered no excuses at his court martial except to say that he was upset by gunfire.[21]

At Question Time in the House of Commons in December, 1917, the Under-Secretary of State for War was asked by a Labour Member to ensure that no soldier who had been seriously wounded or invalided with shell-shock would ever be executed, but the Minister replied that he was not in a position to give effect to such a proposal.[22] A Conservative Member, a retired General, then asked him if it was not a universal practice at courts martial for "a most complete and exhaustive report to be called for" after a death sentence had been passed, so that it would be "practically impossible for any man to be executed who has suffered from shell-shock". The Minister agreed and added that in all the cases which had been brought to his notice the courts had given most careful attention to the reports on the prisoners.[23]

Whether the Under-Secretary had intended to mislead the House or had done so inadvertently, the truth of the matter was that during the previous four months General Haig had twice confirmed death sentences on soldiers whose court-martial papers clearly revealed that they had been treated in hospital for shell-shock. The first case was that of the 21-year-old private in the Royal Scots Fusiliers, which Philip Snowden had raised in the House of Commons, and who had been executed on 29 August. The second man, a private in his mid-twenties serving in the East Yorkshire Regiment, had been invalided home with shell-shock after being buried by earth when a shell had exploded near him in September, 1916. He had been back with his battalion for about six months before he deserted at the end of October, 1917. At his court martial he attributed the offence to his nerves. "I always shake from head to foot when I go into the trenches," he said. Although he was sentenced to death, the members of the Court were obviously worried about their decision as they noted on the file that the prisoner had had nobody to defend him, and that they had called for a medical report but none had been available. The Commander-in-Chief had not shared their disquiet. He had confirmed the death sentence without obtaining any further information and the soldier was shot on 28 December.[24]

Early in 1918 General Haig again confirmed a death sentence on a private when the court-martial papers showed that he had been treated for shell-shock. The soldier was a French-Canadian who had enlisted in August, 1914, in the Seaforth Highlanders. He had been admitted to hospital with shell-shock during the summer of 1917 and had deserted the following November. He was shot on 9 March, 1918.[25]

Combat fatigue was rarely regarded as a ground for clemency at the trials of deserters in the BEF. A 32-year-old regular soldier who went absent from the trenches during the Passchendaele campaign had come out to France with his battalion in September, 1914, and, apart from two occasions when he was recovering from minor wounds, had served with them ever since. He said in his defence, "My nerves are completely broken down. I suffer pains in the head when in the line. Sometimes I don't know what I'm doing." He was executed on 23 September, 1917.[26] Another private, who was 19 at the time of his execution, had deserted at the beginning of the Passchendaele offensive. After enlisting in the Army as a volunteer he had been

102

graded as unfit for active service owing to his neurotic condition. Later he was posted to an infantry battalion in France and had remained with them for fifteen months before going absent. At his trial he put in a written statement in which he stated that the reason for his desertion was that he could not stand the strain of shellfire any longer because of the bad state of his nerves.[27]

Chapter 14

Even during the final year of the First World War the condition known as "shell-shock" was still regarded by many people in Britain with suspicion and contempt. In the eyes of the War Office a man was either wounded or well unless he had some officially authorized disease, said Siegfried Sassoon. "Damage inflicted on the mind did not count as an illness. If 'war neuroses' were indiscriminately encouraged half the expeditionary force might go sick with a touch of neurasthenia." Dr Rivers, the consultant looking after Sassoon at Craiglockhart War Hospital, told him that the local Director of Medical Services had asserted that he never had and never would recognize the existence of such a thing as shell-shock.[1]

With the shortage of manpower as a perpetual problem, the War Office had reason for concern at the number of soldiers breaking down with nervous illnesses. The official casualty figures show that there were 28,533 cases of shell-shock reported in France up to the end of 1917.[2] These were all men who had been graded as "shell-shock wounded"; if those who had been classified as "shell-shock sick" were included the total could probably be doubled, and it amounted to more than the numerical strength of more than two complete infantry divisions.

The medical officers of units in the line did their best to keep down the number of reported shell-shock casualties. Dr Harold Dearden, who had served with the RAMC on the Western Front, said that, whenever a soldier reported sick in or near the trenches, the average MO endeavoured to prove that there was nothing whatever wrong with him.[3] This was confirmed in the report of the War Office inquiry into shell-shock published in 1922 which said:

104

Medical regimental officers of experience have told us that it was a practical impossibility in the most forward areas during active fighting to distinguish between the acute emotional disturbances due to excessive fear, and a voluntary exaggeration of the normal reactions of fear, and malingering . . . Many officers refused to acknowledge the existence of shell-shock in the firing line and were profoundly sceptical of the genuineness of many cases.[4]

This scepticism regarding shell-shock was particularly prevalent among staff officers. Dr H.W. Hills recalled the reception he received in the spring of 1918 when he arrived at the headquarters of the Fourth Army to take up his duties as the neurological consultant. He was the first medical officer to hold this appointment and he was immediately asked what his function would be. His reply that a neurologist was someone who had made a special study of the nervous system was greeted with derisive laughter. It was made clear to him that his new companions considered it quite unnecessary to have a medical report prepared for a soldier convicted of cowardice or desertion. One of them remarked, "If a man lets his comrades down he ought to be shot. If he's a loony, so much the better. What's the good of loonies anyway?" Another officer told him, "We like you, but we don't like your circus." Dr Hills had been greatly concerned about soldiers who were mental defectives, as in his opinion they should not have been in the front line at all. He said that, when giving medical evidence at the trials of such men, he had always found it difficult to convince the members of the Court that a grown man could have the mind and the insecurity of a child, which would make him the first to break down in the stress of battle. It seems that Dr Hills was acquiring a reputation for being too soft-hearted with the sick as he received a message "from High Up" complaining that he was sending far too many patients back to hospitals at the base and reminding him that in view of the shortage of manpower he must return more soldiers to their units as quickly as possible.[5]

The Americans appreciated more than the British the need for segregating the men who were mentally unstable, either at the recruitment centres or in the mobilization camps. The official statistics show that approximately 2 per cent of all army recruits were rejected on psychological grounds at their initial screening and the remainder were subjected to special examinations during elementary training for the detection of those who were neuropathically or psychopathically unsuitable for military service. These endeavours were not wholly successful and on 15 July, 1918, General Pershing, found it necessary to send the following cable to the Chief of Staff in Washington:

> Prevalence of mental disorders in replacement troops recently received suggests urgent importance of intensive efforts in eliminating mentally unfit from new draft prior to departure from the United States.[6]

The presence of a psychiatrist in every combat division of the American Expeditionary Force made it much easier to start the treatment of shell-shocked soldiers very close to the front line. American casualties were usually taken in the first place to a triage, an advanced field hospital. Sometimes as many as 80 per cent of the slightly shell-shocked men admitted to a triage could be sent back to their units within a few days. Approximately 65 per cent of those who were treated at divisional hospitals were subsequently returned to duty. It would seem extremely probable that a high proportion of these patients were simply affected by battle exhaustion, which would account for the rapidity of their recoveries. Behind the triages and the divisional hospitals there were a group of neurological hospitals and one special hospital for victims of war neuroses.[7]

On 15 January, 1918, the Chief Surgeon of the American Expeditionary Forces issued an order setting out the duties and responsibilities of all medical officers who were detailed to work as psychiatrists. He stated:

> It is essential for all such officers to bear in mind the prime necessity of preserving, or restoring for military duty, as many as possible of the officers and enlisted men who may be brought to their attention. On the other hand, they should recommend the evacuation, with the least practicable delay, of all persons likely to continue ineffective or likely to endanger the morale of the organizations of which they are a part. This is particularly true in the case of functional nervous disorders,

106

loosely grouped under the term "shell-shock", but more properly designated as war neuroses.[8]

The Americans adopted a more understanding attitude than the British towards their shell-shocked men at the Front and treated them less harshly when they committed offences due wholly or partially to the state of their nerves. Although the death sentence could be passed by American courts martial for such military offences as disobedience, desertion and misbehaviour before the enemy, no soldiers were ever executed for any of these offences throughout the war.

The number of psychiatrists in the United States Army grew rapidly and before the end of the war had reached a total of 693, of whom 263 were serving overseas. At first a great many senior officers in the American Expeditionary Force were very dubious about their presence and their rôle, but in due course they were fully accepted.[9] No doubt this change of opinion was partly influenced by the fact that the psychiatrists were being so successful in the treatment of their patients. The medical records for the American forces, issued after the Armistice, showed that 25 per cent of the officers and 61 per cent of the enlisted men who had been treated for psychiatric disorders were returned to full duty in the line.[10] Only 4,039 of the cases had been considered so serious that they had to be sent back to the United States.[11] These figures include, of course, a high proportion of soldiers who were suffering from the mildest forms of war neurosis. In many instances it was found that once a patient had been removed from danger, and properly rested, he would recover very quickly. Physicians also believed that reassurance and encouragement played an important part in the curative process.

In British hospitals the methods of treating war neurosis victims had undergone a radical change. An editorial in the *British Medical Journal* in June, 1917, observed that during the early stages of the war most doctors had believed that shell-shock could best be cured by bed-rest, a full diet, sedatives and electric shocks. Patients who were merely afflicted with anxiety disorders often responded so favourably to this routine that after a few weeks or a few months they became fit enough for non-combat duties, and sometimes even for active service. However, those suffering from perceptible physical symptoms, such as paralysis, tremors, or lack of balance, had seldom shown much improvement.[12] Dr W.H.R. Rivers, one of the leading British authorities on war neurosis, said in 1918 that these early forms of treatment had concentrated too much on bodily disabilities and had ignored the psychological inception of the illness. Although the results had been beneficial in a number of cases, he had noticed that all too often "they merely accentuated the disease, and even produced new manifestations, by encouraging the patient to believe in the physical character of his condition."[13]

Dr Rivers disagreed with the view that a shell-shocked soldier should be urged to forget the occurrences on the battlefield. In a paper he read to the Edinburgh Pathological Club in March, 1917, he said that the usual advice given to patients in the past had been that they should put their war experiences out of their minds and should try not to think about them. But "during the solitude and pain of the night" their recollections would come flooding back to them uncontrollably. It was far better that the patient should be encouraged to face up to his memories with resolution:

> We should point out to him that such an experience as that of which he had been the subject can never be thrust wholly out of his life, though it may be possible to put it out of sight and cover it up so it may seem to be forgotten. His experience should be talked over in all its bearings. Its good side should be emphasized for it is characteristic of the painful experience of warfare that it usually has a good, or even a noble side, which in his condition of misery the patient does not see at all, or greatly underestimates . . . The relief afforded to the patient by the process of talking over his painful experience, and by discussing how he can readjust his life to the new conditions, usually gives immense relief and may be followed by a great improvement, or even by the rapid disappearance of his chief symptoms.[14]

Before the war Dr Rivers had been equally eminent as a neurologist and as an anthropologist. Early in 1915 he had become a civilian physician at Moss Side Hospital in Maghull, near Liverpool. Moss Side, formerly used as a convalescent home for children from workhouses, had been taken over in December, 1914, as the Merseyside

108

Red Cross Hospital for shell-shocked soldiers. It had soon attracted to its medical staff a group of gifted and imaginative consultants who had been specializing in mental and nervous illness and their work at the hospital had played a prominent part in the new perception of the psychological nature of war neurosis. In January, 1916, Rivers, then a Captain in the Royal Army Medical Corps, was transferred to Craiglockhart War Hospital, just outside Edinburgh, where all the patients were army officers who had broken down during the fighting on the Western Front. Rivers carried on there with the methods which he and others had been using so effectively at Moss Side. He believed, in particular, that the successful treatment of war neurosis required a close relationship between the physician and the patient; further, that the patient must have a true understanding of his condition and he must have the ability to confront it courageously.[15]

As the war had progressed the medical facilities in Britain for the reception of shell-shock casualties from the Front had improved immeasurably. By 1918 there were more than twenty special hospitals in various parts of the country with a total of around 6,000 beds where patients could be treated. The majority of these temporary hospitals were converted lunatic asylums, whose former inmates had been moved to other institutions before the military took them over. The staffs were generally efficient and comparatively well trained.[16] Only the worst cases of war neurosis were sent home at that time, the others being kept at the army hospitals in France. The most difficult patients to manage from the point of view of the medical authorities were probably those who were classed as suffering from "acute confusional insanity". When they were first admitted to a ward, according to the official medical history of the Great War, they were usually in such a wildly excited condition that they needed to be tied into their beds, and even then they continued to struggle and shout, sometimes for as much as two or three days. As a rule they were hostile and suspicious and they often thought the staff were Germans in disguise. At the end of several weeks they would "still show signs of confusion, persistent hallucinations, ideas of persecution, and other symptoms."[17]

During the latter months of 1917 the majority of the officers and men reporting sick with shell-shock in the BEF were suffering from simple battle exhaustion. They were kept for treatment in the advanced hospitals and never left the army area. After two or three weeks rest and care around 55 per cent were returned to their units for normal duty. A relatively small proportion of the patients, on average about 16 per cent, were sent back to the base, and about 10 per cent were ultimately evacuated to England.[18]

It might be supposed that in view of the growing awareness of the nature of war neurosis and the more sympathetic attitude being adopted to those who had succumbed to it, a number of men would have faked the better-known symptoms of the disorder to escape from service at the Front. However, the official medical history of the war stated that the incidence of "true malingering" was rare and could only be established with certainty in very few instances. One soldier tried to feign deaf-mutism, another blindness, and several more loss of memory, but in all these cases the deceptions were discovered. Sometimes a man who was mildly affected by war neurosis would pretend to be worse than he really was and it would be difficult for the doctors to determine the extent to which he was exaggerating his symptoms.[19]

An interesting account of the life of the officer-patients at Craiglockhart War Hospital was given by Siegfried Sassoon in his book *Sherston's Progress*, which also provided an informative study of the personality of Dr Rivers and his skills as a counsellor. Sassoon was not suffering from war neurosis, and the reason for his being sent to Craiglockhart was a strange one. He came from an aristocratic background and, after leaving Cambridge, had chosen to live the life of a cultivated gentleman, hunting, playing cricket, collecting books and occasionally writing poetry. Soon after the outbreak of war he enlisted as a trooper in a county cavalry regiment and at the beginning of 1915 he was commissioned in the Royal Welch Fusiliers. He was posted to the BEF and he soon became known as a remarkably brave officer. He was awarded the MC for going out into no-man's-land under heavy fire to bring back a wounded soldier, and it was said that he was unsuccessfully recommended for the VC for his gallantry during an attack. He had served in France with his battalion until April, 1917, when he was slightly wounded. While he was convalescing in England he had become distrustful of the allied war aims and he had come to the conclusion that the fighting, with its wholesale slaughter and all its misery, should be ended. Encouraged by pacifist friends he wrote and circulated a declaration starting:

110

I am making this statement as an act of wilful defiance of military authority, because I believe that the War is being deliberately prolonged by those who have the power to end it. I am a soldier, convinced that I am acting on behalf of soldiers. I believe that the War, upon which I entered as a war of defence and liberation, has now become a war of aggression and conquest. I believe that the purposes for which I and my fellow soldiers entered upon this War should have been so clearly stated as to have made it impossible to change them, and that, had this been done, the objects which actuated us would now be attainable by negotiation. I have seen and endured the sufferings of the troops, and I can no longer be a party to prolong those sufferings for ends which I believe to be evil and unjust.[20]

Sassoon had expected to be court-martialled for his conduct, but the military authorities directed him to appear before a Special Medical Board. He refused to do so and he was warned that if he persisted with his disobedience he would be shut up in a lunatic asylum for the rest of the war. In view of this threat he gave way. After questioning Sassoon about the motives for his declaration, the Medical Board decided that he was suffering from shell-shock and ordered that he should go to Craiglockhart for treatment.[21]

Siegfried Sassoon has described Craiglockhart as having the melancholy atmosphere of a decayed hydro. The place, he said, was a live museum of war neuroses; "in other words, the hospital contained about 150 officers who had been either shattered or considerably shaken by their war experience." No money had been spent on decorating the rooms because the War Office still regarded war hospitals for nervous disorders as being experimental and viewed them with a certain amount of suspicion since "the delicate problem of 'lead-swingers' was involved". Sassoon found his main problem was how to pass the time and, as there was nothing the matter with him, he spent most of his days at Craiglockhart playing golf. He felt that he was a healthy young officer "dumped down among nurses and nervous wrecks". He found the hospital particularly oppressive during the night when so many of the insomnia-ridden patients spent half the night smoking in their bedrooms.

111

One became conscious that the place was full of men whose slumbers were morbid and terrifying – men muttering uneasily or suddenly crying out in their sleep. Around me was that underworld of dreams haunted by submerged memories of warfare . . . each man was back in his doomed sector of a horror-stricken Front Line, where the panic and stampede of some ghastly experience was re-enacted among the livid faces of the dead.[22]

As soon as he arrived at Craiglockhart Sassoon was put under the care of Dr Rivers, for whom he formed an enormous admiration and respect. At their first meeting Rivers won him over completely. "There was never any doubt about my liking him," Sassoon wrote. "He made me feel safe at once, and seemed to know all about me. What he didn't know he soon found out."[23]

Rivers had told Sassoon that, although he most certainly was not suffering from shell-shock, the military authorities intended to keep him at Craiglockhart until the end of the war if he persisted with his pacifist attitude. It was significant, perhaps, that the Under-Secretary for War had stated in the House of Commons that Sassoon had undergone a nervous breakdown before issuing his statement, and he was not responsible for his actions.[24]

Sassoon knew that Rivers, whom he called his "father-confessor", was trying to encourage him to abandon his pacifism, and after spending three months at the hospital he agreed to do so. He appeared before another Medical Board which pronounced him to be sufficiently recovered to return to active service. On his final morning at Craiglockhart Siegfried Sassoon said goodbye to Dr. Rivers. He has described his reactions:

Shutting the door of his room for the last time, I left behind me someone who had helped and understood me more than anyone I had ever known. Much as he disliked speeding me back to the trenches, he realized that it was my only way out. And the longer I live the more right I know him to have been.[25]

During his time at Craiglockhart Siegfried Sassoon formed a close friendship with a fellow-patient, Wilfred Owen, who was destined, like

Sassoon, to achieve renown for his wartime poetry. Owen, then aged 24 and unknown, had been affected by war neurosis after a shell had exploded close to him on the Western Front the previous April. Throughout the summer he was afflicted, like so many of the other patients at Craiglockhart, with insomnia and nightmares. It is known that while they were together in the hospital Sassoon encouraged Owen to keep on writing and sometimes suggested alterations to improve his verse.[26]

After leaving Craiglockhart Siegfried Sassoon was posted to Palestine for a few months before returning to France. He received a head-wound in July, 1918, which ended his active service. Wilfred Owen rejoined his battalion in France in August, 1918. He was killed the following November, exactly a week before the Armistice.

Chapter 15

At the beginning of 1918 the German Army on the Western Front was superior to the combined forces of the Allies both in manpower and artillery. The Russian withdrawal from the war during the previous year had made it possible for Germany to transfer all her troops and weaponry from the eastern front to concentrate her entire military strength in France and Belgium. Throughout January and February allied intelligence sources were receiving reports that a massive German offensive was imminent, aimed either at the occupation of the Channel ports or the capture of Paris.

Haig had informed the War Office that he would be requiring 615,000 more men for his operations in the coming months, but he had been told he could expect little more than 100,000, and that most of them would be 18-year-old conscripts who had never been in action before.

Rumours were continuing to circulate in Britain about the frequency with which executions were taking place in the BEF for purely military offences and disquiet was mounting, but the Government adamantly refused to disclose any details. At Question Time in the House of Commons on 19 February, 1918, the Labour MP Philip Snowden inquired whether at courts martial for cowardice and desertion medical evidence that the accused soldiers were not suffering from shell-shock was always given on oath and was always subject to cross-examination. The Under-Secretary of State for War assured him that the answer was "yes" to both questions.[1] Once again the House was misled. At none of the trials for cowardice or desertion for which the records are still extant was such evidence given. In fact, if the accused men underwent medical boards at all in relation to their mental condition, these took place after the court-martial proceedings were finished. The Under-Secretary had gone on to say that whenever there was the least suspicion of shell-shock every possible medical advice was obtained. He "deeply resented" the suggestion made by another Labour MP that there had been occasions when soldiers suffering from shell-shock were executed and he demanded that the allegation should be withdrawn.[2]

When the House was debating the Army Estimates later the same day the Under-Secretary of State for War stated categorically that he had not been able to discover a single case of a man being executed when it was proved that he had been wounded or shell-shocked in the past.[3]

A small number of Labour members were not yet satisfied and the subject was raised again on several occasions during the next few weeks. On 14 March, during a debate on the Consolidated Fund Bill, the Under-Secretary of State for War agreed that shell-shock should not be associated with cowardice. "One has come across case after case," he went on, "of the most gallant fellows who ever drew breath, whose nerves are so badly shattered that only half of their whole bodily strength and mental vigour remains." To show how much care was taken in the BEF to prevent shell-shocked soldiers from being executed for military offences, he read to the House part of a letter he had received from the Commander-in-Chief. Haig had written:

> When a man has been sentenced to death, if at any time any doubt had been raised as to his responsibility for his actions, or if the suggestion has been advanced that he has suffered from neurasthenia or shell-shock, orders are issued for him to be examined by a Medical Board which expresses an opinion as to his sanity, and as to whether he should be held responsible for his actions. One of the members of this board is always a medical officer of neurological experience. The sentence of death is not carried out in the case of such a man unless the Medical Board expresses the positive opinion that he is to be held responsible for his actions.[4]

An Army Order, which was issued about this time, stated that "when a man accused of desertion, etc., pleaded that he was suffering or had

115

suffered from shell-shock, he is to be admitted to the special army N.Y.D.N. centre for observation".[5] The editors of *The Official Medical History of the War* commented that in marked cases of nervous disorder there was no difficulty in certifying that such men were sick and should be admitted to hospital. Where, however, a soldier was in a slightly neurasthenic state the case became far more difficult. If men were admitted for observation under the Army Order they were detained at the Centre for a period of at least four weeks, during which time they were interviewed by a doctor once or twice every day, and were medically examined on three or four separate occasions. Finally, reports on them were submitted to their respective army headquarters for use at their courts martial. In the opinion of the editors "only a few of the cases of desertion were caused by mental deficiency, minor epilepsy, delusional insanity and dementia," although there were occasional instances of soldiers in the front line affected genuinely by loss of awareness and wandering off in a dazed condition.[6]

At first light on 21 March, 1918, the Germans began a well-prepared all-out offensive which was intended to drive back the BEF to the Channel coast. After a hurricane bombardment with 4,000 guns the German infantry poured across no-man's-land under cover of a thick morning mist. Their attack was successful in practically every sector of a 40-mile British front. South of the River Somme General Gough's heavily-defeated Fifth Army retreated in confusion, abandoning vast quantities of artillery, ammunition and stores. As the onslaught surged forward the Allied position became increasingly grave. New drafts of half-trained troops were rushed out from England and every man who could possibly be spared from the British forces in Italy, Salonika and Palestine was hurriedly transferred to France. General Pétain, the French Commander-in-Chief, fearing a German thrust against Paris, was unable to render much assistance, but General Pershing placed all the American divisions in the AEF at the disposal of the Allies.

On 11 April, Haig issued a Special Order of the Day:

There is no other course open to us but to fight it out. Every position must be held to the last man: there must be no retirement. With our backs to the wall and believing in the justice of our cause each one of us must fight on to the end.

Since the start of the German offensive the previous month the BEF had sustained more than 178,000 casualties, out of whom over 70,000 officers and men had been killed. Despite their appalling losses the British managed eventually to stabilize their line and, in compliance with the orders from their Commander-in-Chief, they stood fast and beat back every new German attack.

On 27 May the Germans opened another major offensive, this time against the French. In three days they had reached the banks of the River Marne and had approached within striking distance of Paris. The French hung on desperately and in mid-July, with the help of the Americans, they carried out a surprise assault which repelled the Germans from nearly all their foremost positions. Sensing that the tide of fortune may have turned in their favour, the Allies went into the attack all along the line on 8 August. They achieved a notable victory; the German Official Monograph described it as the greatest defeat their Army had suffered since the beginning of the war. Shortly afterwards the Kaiser told one of his senior Generals, "We have nearly reached the limits of our powers of resistance. The war must be ended."[7]

By then the British and French Divisions on the Western Front were filled with half-trained youths and inexperienced NCOs. The German Army, too, was drawing its reinforcements from the very young, the physically unfit and the middle-aged. The Allies continued to press forward their attack, but the Germans, becoming increasingly dispirited and demoralized, still fought on as they retreated. They made their final stand on the heavily fortified Hindenburg Line, and when this was broken by the Allies at the beginning of October they resumed their withdrawal. A German General complained in a confidential letter about the shattered morale of his troops. "They surrender in hordes," he wrote, "whenever the enemy attacks, and thousands of plunderers infest the districts round the bases. We have no prepared lines and no more can be dug."[8]

In early November Marshal von Hindenburg, the Supreme Commander of the German Field Army, informed the Kaiser that the nation's resources were at an end, and that they were left with no alternative but to seek an immediate armistice. The Kaiser agreed with him. The terms of the armistice which was then arranged virtually entailed the unconditional surrender of all the German armed forces on the morning of 11 November, 1918.

The Under-Secretary of State for War had assured the House of Commons that at courts martial for desertion medical evidence was always given on oath that the accused soldiers were not suffering from shell-shock, but this is not borne out in the documents relating to the men who were executed for this offence during 1918. Nor do the documents confirm Haig's assertion that if any doubt had been raised regarding a condemned soldier's responsibility for his actions it was the invariable practice to have him examined by a Medical Board.

At this stage of the war the soldiers who had fought on the Western Front for months, possibly for years on end, were particularly likely to be affected by war neurosis. Great care should have been taken before deciding that such men were entirely culpable for their behaviour. On 12 January, 1918, a 21-year-old private in the Royal Inniskilling Fusiliers was tried for deserting two months previously. He did not deny going absent and could only say in his defence, "My nerves got the better of me". The court was told that he was a volunteer who had landed in France in August, 1914. Even though this was his second desertion, no medical evidence was called and he was not medically examined before he was executed on 24 January.[9] A similar claim that the fighting had affected the state of his nerves was made by a 26-year-old private in the Buffs who was shot on 28 August. No medical evidence was given in this case either.[10]

A soldier, court-martialled for desertion on 30 August, 1918, gave evidence that he was suffering from pains in the head and had phases of loss of memory. The details of his military career which came out at this trial were that he had enlisted as a volunteer at the age of 25 and had served with the BEF since June, 1915. He was wounded in 1916 and subsequently had been convicted of desertion and of causing a self-inflicted wound. It may have been on account of his previous offences that the court did not take his evidence seriously. At any rate, he was never medically examined before his execution on 10 September.[11]

Another private who should have undergone a medical examination

118

was executed for desertion two days later. He was a 22-year-old Irishman serving with the Machine Gun Corps. He too had enlisted as a volunteer in 1915 and had been wounded at the end of 1916. At his trial he had declined either to give evidence or to make a statement. Even though he had two previous convictions for desertion and was described as a very bad soldier, the case against him was highly unsatisfactory as the prosecution called no medical witness who could say that he had been accountable for his behaviour at the time he went absent. The Court was told that he had been a member of a working party in the front line. Some shells had exploded close to them and straightaway the Irishman had wandered off. He had not been seen again until five days later when he had reported to the military police in the base area and had asked them for help in finding his way back to his unit.[12]

The last British soldier to be shot at dawn for desertion in the First World War was executed on 7 November, 1918, four days before the Armistice. He had said in his defence that both his mother and father had died in lunatic asylums and that he himself had suffered from mental trouble. The Court had neither adjourned for further enquiries to be made, nor thought it desirable to hear medical evidence before imposing a death sentence on him.[13]

Field Marshal Haig had authorized all these executions, despite his assertion to the Under-Secretary of State for War that if any doubt had arisen about a condemned soldier's mental condition he was always examined by a Medical Board to make sure that he had been responsible for his actions.

In October, 1917, Lieut-Colonel Myers, the Consultant Neurologist to the BEF, had been recalled to England, and the control of the Army Centres for Nervous Disorders in France was passed to Lieut-Colonel Gordon Holmes, the BEF's Consultant Psychologist. There was then a forward Centre in each Army area and the Adjutant-General's order still applied that, directly a patient was admitted to one of them, his Commanding Officer would be consulted confidentially to ascertain whether he should be graded as "shell-shock wounded" or as "shell-shock sick". If the patient had been blown up or buried by the blast of an exploding shell the choice was a comparatively easy one, but when he had simply broken down under the strain of trench warfare the decision would rest solely on the arbitrary opinion of his Commanding

119

Officer. The reason for this absurd division of shell-shock patients into two distinct groups was explained by the Editors of *The Official Medical History of the War*:

> The position taken up by the military authorities may be summed up thus. The psycho-neuroses cannot be ignored. Certain cases require medical care. The subject is, however, so bound up with the maintenance of morale in the army that every soldier who is non-effective owing to nervous break-down must be made the subject of careful enquiry.[14]

During 1917 and 1918 an average of 40 per cent of the shell-shock patients admitted to the Army Centres for Nervous diseases in France were classified as "wounded" and 60 per cent as "sick".[15]

In September, 1918, it was decided that from then on no patient could be categorized as "shell-shock wounded" while he was still serving in France. If his condition was sufficiently serious for him to be returned to England he would be examined in due course by a Neurological Board at one of the Special Centres in the United Kingdom, which would consider all the circumstances of his break-down and would determine whether or not it should be classed as a wound.[16]

By June, 1918, there were nineteen special military hospitals in England and Scotland for the treatment of war neuroses. Six of them provided accommodation for 1,200 officers and the remainder had accommodation for 4,500 other ranks. In addition, if there was an overflow of cases, an extra 400 beds could be available at various central hospitals. A new method for the disposal of neurasthenic casualties had been established. When they no longer required hospital treatment a Neurological Board decided if they were fit for any further military service. Those who were well enough to remain in the army were sent on leave and were then posted to a home-based unit. Their medical history sheets were endorsed in red ink with a note that they were neurasthenics and were not to be sent overseas again before they had been re-boarded. Six months after their discharge from hospital they appeared before another board for a further examination.[17]

The military historian John Keegan has commented that any

statistics showing the proportion of psychiatric casualties to the casualties due to wounds in the First World War still remain hidden.[18] With regard to the British Army, *The Official Medical History of the War*, published in 1923, contained details of "shell-shock cases reported as battle casualties" on the Western Front between September, 1914, and December, 1917.[19] The number given is 28,533. These were men, of course, whose condition was adjudged by their Commanding Officers as having been caused by the traumatic experiences they had undergone in the line; the Editors believed that if cases designated as "shell-shock sick" had been included the total would be in the region of 80,000.[20] It was known that in February, 1921, approximately 65,000 ex-soldiers were drawing disability pensions on account of neurasthenic and other related conditions arising out of the recently-ended war; 14,771 of them were still being treated in hospital. At the end of 1922 the number of neurasthenic pensioners had fallen to about 50,000 but the total in hospital had increased to 16,771. "It is to be feared," the Editors wrote, "that a large proportion of them will never recover their full mental capacity."[21] Fresh cases of war neurosis were occurring continuously during the post-war years and in March, 1939, almost twenty-one years after the Armistice, some 120,000 ex-servicemen were either receiving pensions or had been paid a final award for war-related "primary psychiatric disability". In that year they accounted for 15 percent of all the disabled pensioners from the 1914–1918 War.[22] According to a correspondent in *The Lancet* many of the men who had recovered sufficiently to take up employment were troubled by a feeling of insecurity and by a suspicion that their nervous symptoms were being derided by other people.[23]

A total of 69,394 men in the American Expeditionary Force were disabled by neuropsychiatric disorders during the First World War.[24] Dr Thomas Salmon, who had done such useful work in preparing the AEF for the reception and treatment of war neurosis casualties, addressed the American Red Cross Convention at Columbus, Ohio, in October, 1921, on some of the problems which had confronted this type of pensioner since the Armistice.[25] A strange lethargy had fallen on the United States of America when the war was over, he said, combined with a mood of irritability. Some day the historian, the political economist and the sociologist would discover the deep underlying reasons "that led the richest nation on the earth to permit a period of almost unbelievable neglect of its disabled defenders to follow the successful termination of its greatest war." There were at that time 28,535 disabled ex-servicemen receiving hospital care at the expense of the Government, he went on, and of these 7,804 or 27 per cent, were suffering from neuropsychiatric illness. Their treatment would extend over many months, or even years, and they would continue to suffer from their disorders for the rest of their lives. They required special types of hospital for successful treatment and he urged the authorities to provide them. It was both unscientific and inhumane to care for mental patients for long periods in general hospitals where their presence at games and entertainments, and even in common mess halls, was resented by the other patients. Dr Salmon believed that three years after the Armistice there were definite signs of a re-awakening of public concern about the welfare of disabled veterans and there was a planned programme, although an inadequate one, for the construction of new hospitals. Certain people, he said, were bound to object to the expense involved, but those who complained about the burden of caring for the war-disabled were unworthy of being allowed to bear that burden at all.[26] In fact, over the next twenty years the United States Government was to spend a considerable amount of money on the treatment and welfare of ex-servicemen with psychiatric disabilities.[27]

In the course of his talk at Columbus Dr Salmon had alluded to the long-term treatment which would be required by many of the pensioners suffering from war neuroses.[28] A follow-up study, carried out on 760 of these men after the war, showed that in 1920 more than 60 per cent were troubled with symptoms of psychotic illness and nearly 40 per cent were unfit for any form of employment. The position in 1925 was that 60 per cent were still affected with varying degrees of nervous anxiety, but the number who were unemployable had fallen to 20 per cent.[29]

The 1914–1918 war marked a turning-point in the public attitude to war neurosis. The vast number of "shell-shocked" veterans, the greater understanding of the factors which had led to their condition, and the realization that even the bravest of men had a limit to their fortitude, had nullified the stigma of breaking down in battle. Perhaps it was indicative of this awareness that in 1919 a new charity called Combat Stress was founded in London for the purpose of helping men

122

and women of all ranks who had developed a psychiatric illness while serving in the Armed Forces or the Merchant Navy. In their appeal literature, the charity used the telling phrase "They tried to give more than they could," and it adopted Rudyard Kipling's evocative stanza:

They broke his body and his mind,
And yet they made him live,
They asked more from My Mother's son
Than any man could give.[30]

Chapter 16

In the House of Lords on 28 April, 1920, Lord Southborough urged the Government to set up an Enquiry into the various forms of hysteria, commonly called "shell-shock", which had affected so many soldiers in the recently-ended war, with particular attention being paid to the death penalty imposed by courts martial on men charged with cowardice.[1]

For the whole war, said Lord Southborough, the British people had been confronted with "the sinister and terrible disorder of shell-shock". At first they had been assured that it was specifically associated with the particular conditions under which the Army was fighting. Now, however, the consensus of opinion in Britain, France and America was that soldiers who were said to have been shell-shocked were, in reality, suffering from different types of hysteria or traumatic neurosis which were common and well-known in civil life. It was only to be expected, he added, that some of the boys who had been taken from their peacetime occupations and had suddenly been exposed "to the inferno of fire, noise, blood, and death" would crack up; it was amazing that the vast majority of them had remained firm and sound in mind and body until the Armistice.

Lord Southborough said that he recognized the anxiety of the Generals and the perplexity of the members of courts martial when confronted by shell-shock cases. They were principally concerned with the maintenance of discipline and fighting efficiency. On the other hand, soldiers suffering from acute hysteria might have undergone a complete loss of will-power and have had no control over their actions. He wondered whether wartime courts martial had been empowered to consider the condition of the accused man's mind at the moment he

124

had committed his offence. In the early months of the war, before the true nature of shell-shock was known, he feared that dreadful things might have happened to men who were not really responsible for their behaviour.

Lord Southborough was then 60. He had been a peer since 1917, having occupied a number of senior positions in the Civil Service. He never took part in political debates in the House of Lords, where he spoke very rarely and mainly about issues of public concern.

Among the peers who supported Lord Southborough's proposal was Lord Horne, who had commanded the First Army on the Western Front from the autumn of 1916 until the end of the war. He admitted that in the early days of the war there may have been court-martial cases "where injustice led to the extreme penalty being enforced", but in practice, he said, if there was the slightest suspicion that an offence had been committed by a soldier who was suffering from "any of the forms of hysteria which are included under the term 'shell-shock'", he could confidently state that the sentence was never confirmed until the accused had been placed under medical observation.

At the close of the discussion Viscount Peel, the Under-Secretary of State for War, said that the Government took the view that great advantages might be derived from an Enquiry such as had been suggested by Lord Southborough, with the proviso that it would be very wrong and detrimental to discipline if there was to be an investigation of court-martial cases which had already been settled.

A War Office Committee of Enquiry into "Shell-Shock" was appointed four months later under the chairmanship of Lord Southborough. There were fifteen members, eleven of whom had medical qualifications and two of whom were Members of Parliament. The terms of reference submitted to them by the Army Council were:

> To consider the different types of hysteria and traumatic neurosis, commonly called "shell-shock"; to collate the expert knowledge derived by the service medical authorities and the medical profession from the experience of the war, with a view to recording for future use the ascertained facts as to its origins, nature, and remedial treatment, and to advise whether by military training or education, some scientific method of guarding against its occurrence can be devised.[2]

The Committee met for the first time early in September, 1920, and continued in session until the summer of 1922. During this period they held forty-one sittings and heard evidence from fifty-nine witnesses, including leading neurologists, senior service officers and others who had had experience as doctors or as soldiers on the Western Front. Finally, they produced a report which was probably one of the most reasoned and comprehensive studies of war neurosis that had ever been compiled.[3]

From the outset of their meetings the Committee had agreed that the description "shell-shock" was a gross misnomer for the disorders to which it had been applied. In spite of this, as the word "shell-shock" appeared in their Terms of Reference and was already well-established with the general public, they decided to use it in their Report, but always to print it in inverted commas.

At the start of their deliberations the Committee had wished to know if there was any history of war neurosis in earlier wars. They asked John Fortescue, the doyen of military historians at the time, if he could provide them with information on the subject. Fortescue replied that he could not contribute anything which might be of value to their researches. The writers about the wars of the past occasionally mentioned details which bore upon the question, he said, but their narratives were generally composed some time after the event and were not too trustworthy. During the campaigns of the nineteenth century, however, it was not unknown for soldiers to be seriously shaken-up by an explosion when a building was being demolished.

It is surprising that Fortescue did not refer to nostalgia, soldiers' irritable heart, or windage. He went on to say:

> No doubt there were men who, from one cause or another, broke down in every campaign; and I have little doubt that this was one of the causes that led to desertion. But such breaks down, when they are recorded, are not very sympathetically treated, and unless a man has proved himself of good courage earlier in action, are dismissed as not differing greatly from cowardice. Of course, numbers of men went out of their minds in old campaigns as they still do.[4]

126

Fortescue was of the opinion that the bravest man could not endure to be under fire for more than a certain number of consecutive days, even if the fire was not particularly heavy.

The Committee would have liked to obtain reliable statistics of the number of shell-shock cases during the 1914–1918 War but this information was not available. Many of the relevant records had been lost and other statistical details were buried in the archives of the War Office and other Government Departments and were inaccessible.[5]

In their report the Committee said that an important part of their task had been to ascertain what "shell-shock" was and what it was not. During the early days of the war the term had arisen from the necessity of finding a suitable name "for the number of cases of functional nervous incapacity which were continually occurring among the fighting units". In the popular mind, the Report continued, "shell-shock" signified that the patient had suffered the physical effects of the explosion of missiles, but later, when nervous disorders, neuroses and hysteria were becoming "astoundingly numerous", it was apparent that they originated from other causes than shock from bursting shells. By then the medical profession had realized that the wear and tear of a prolonged campaign of trench warfare, with all its terrible hardships and anxieties, could produce a condition of mind and body which was more appropriately described as "war neurosis". This was, in fact, practically indistinguishable from the forms of neurosis known to every doctor under ordinary conditions of civil life.

The Committee concluded that the cases of war neurosis could be divided into three main classes. First, genuine concussion without any visible wound as the result of a shell-explosion; secondly, emotional shock, which might occur among men with an exceptionally nervous disposition, or might develop slowly as a consequence of prolonged strain and terrifying experiences; and thirdly, nervous and mental exhaustion following a period of incessant stress and hardship.[6]

The medical witnesses who were examined by the Committee were unanimous in their opinion that shell-shock was far less frequently a commotional disturbance resulting from a shell explosion than an emotional disorder due to other factors. Dr Gordon Holmes, who had been the Consultant Neurologist to the BEF, said that investigations carried out at several forward field hospitals had revealed that only an average of between 4 and 10 per cent of the shell-shock cases had originated in commotional shock. Two other neurologists who had served in France had given their own numerical assessments. One of them stated that less than 10 per cent of his shell-shock cases had been caused by concussion, and the other said that, in broad terms, 80 per cent of his cases were due to emotional agitation, 5 per cent to commotional disturbance and the remaining 15 per cent to a mixture of both. A doctor who had been a regimental medical officer with a battalion of the Black Watch said, "I consider that the majority of cases that one meets with on active service are not due to shells at all. The majority are entirely anxiety neurosis . . . I would put commotional cases at 5 per cent, if as much as that."[7]

Dr W.H.R. Rivers, who was then lecturing at Cambridge University, told the Committee that the main factor in shell-shock was stress. The shock of a bursting shell was often the last straw which caused men to break down, but the effects of the explosion had only made a trivial contribution to their disorder. Their stress had been brought about by a variety of causes, including sleeplessness, anxiety, fatigue, responsibility, and battle experiences such as the sight of their friends being killed and mutilated all around them. Dr Rivers said that he never used the word "neurasthenia". What was generally known as "neurasthenia" he preferred to call "anxiety neurosis". Hysteria and anxiety neurosis were combined in the majority of "shell-shock" cases. The hysteria might well be cured and the patient would then develop an anxiety state.[8]

A neurologist who had been in France at the beginning of the war condemned the introduction of the word "shell-shock" as an official term. In those days, he said, soldiers had developed a belief that a bursting shell produced mysterious changes in the nervous system which could destroy their self-control. They had started to regard shell-shock as a specific disease, and new recruits, in action for the first time, were prepared to contract it almost before the first shell had dropped anywhere near them.[9]

Nearly all the neurologists and regimental medical officers who gave evidence before the Committee shared Dr Rivers' opinion that the predominant cause of war neurosis was mental stress. Professor Elliott said that during his time as Consultant Physician to the British Armies in France he had come to the conclusion that this stress was usually the result of a state of persistent or recurring fear which overrode the soldiers' self-control. Other doctors attributed stress to the exhaustion of a man's nervous energy, fatigue, scenes of horror, prolonged responsibility, lengthy service in the front line, the strain and danger of the battlefield and the soldiers' inability to adapt himself to the tension of warfare. A physician who had been the officer-in-charge of an army neurological hospital believed that "no man, however normal he may be at first, is likely to be immune to 'shell-shock'".[10]

Some of the witnesses spoke of the contributory factors which might predispose soldiers to a neurotic condition. A Professor of Physiology at a Welsh university told the Committee that 17 per cent of the men about to go into the front line for the first time were troubled by nightmares and 31 per cent by broken sleep. About 11 per cent of the men who were actually in the line talked, shouted or screamed in their sleep. Dr R.W. Rows, a specialist in war neurosis, said that soldiers could break down under shellfire because they were already in an emotional state, produced by a series of causes, some of them unconnected with the war. "Maybe a letter from home with bad news, his mother dead or something of that sort, which had so upset his control that he can stand the line no longer."[11]

Witnesses said that units were often left in the line until the men were suffering from nervous exhaustion. A doctor who had been working with a field ambulance section during the Somme offensive told of one instance when a Division had gone "over the top" eleven times in a fortnight, and a mass of soldiers went down with shell-shock because they could not take any more. One Medical Officer who had served with an infantry battalion, commented, "I must certainly say that had it not been for the rum ration I do not think we should have won the war."[12]

Even as late as 1920 there were still people in positions of responsibility who had failed to understand the true nature of war neurosis. Lieut-Colonel Hewlett, who had been Inspector of Infantry Training, said in evidence before the Committee that he would define shell-shock as the condition suffered by a soldier after a shell had exploded so close as to "knock him silly". The term had been used quite wrongly to include any man suffering from nerves. Major Adie, a neurologist on the staff of the Ministry of Pensions, said that shell-shock was any state of mind or body, engendered or perpetuated by fear, which renders a soldier less efficient or enables him to evade his duty without fear of being punished. He thought that a man who had simply broken down mentally should not be given a wound stripe, but a man with an obvious commotional shock who had been buried or blown up deserved to have one.[13]

Lord Horne, speaking as an Army Commander, admitted that he had looked with disfavour on any battalion which had had a large number of shell-shock cases, as he considered it to be a sign of poor morale, and poor morale was often due to inefficiency and incompetent training. Dr Gordon Holmes thought that the large increase in the prevalence of shell-shock as the war went on was partly accounted for by the fact that the morale of the troops at the Front was not so high as it had been in the original expeditionary force and many of the men in the new drafts expected to become shell-shocked. Dr Rivers shared the view that battle-stress and morale could be inter-related. "The whole object of military training," he said, "is to produce esprit de corps and other factors which give good morale, and the lack of them is a strong factor in the production of neuroses of certain kinds."[14]

A Consultant Physician in the French Army referred to the fear of poison gas playing a major part in producing nervous disorders on the Western Front. In early stages of the war, he said, gas had been a new and untried weapon with all the terrors of the unknown. Later, when the troops had understood more about it, the dread of a gas-attack had in no way diminished. One reason why it had created so much emotional disturbance was that gas affected the respiratory organs and nothing was more likely to create panic than the idea of being choked; it was akin to being buried alive or being slowly strangled to death.[15]

On the subject of soldiers returning to the front line after being treated for war neurosis, the Committee stated in their Report that several medical witnesses of great experience had told them it was an error to hold too strongly to the view that the men who had suffered from shell-shock were permanently incapable of further active service. It depended on the individual temperament of the man concerned and on the nature of his neurosis. With patients who were merely suffering from exhaustion, the prognosis for the future was fairly good, but in more severe cases there was evidence that they would relapse very soon when they were under fire again. It had been very difficult for the Committee to obtain any accurate figures with regard to the frequency

130

of relapses, as, owing to the constant movement of Divisions, patients did not necessarily return to the same centres and hospitals where they had previously been treated.

Not surprisingly, some of the witnesses who gave evidence found it difficult to accept that war neurosis was a genuine disorder. An infantry colonel referred contemptuously to soldiers going down with "nerve-shock", another name for loss of self-control, which was a disgrace to themselves and to the Army. He was quite certain, he said, that in a pre-war regular regiment if an officer had not broken down in battle very few of his men would have done so. On the Western Front, however, the spirit had been different, and whenever a battalion went into the attack a number of its men remained in their dugouts claiming, quite falsely, that they had been blown up by shells. A cavalry colonel, who had commanded the 5th Lancers in France, considered shell-shock was simply loss of nerve. He attributed its existence to bad officers or the faulty handling of a regiment by the staff. In his opinion, if troops were properly led it could be avoided altogether.[16]

Other Army officers variously defined shell-shock as being, to a large extent, "mental-terror", "loss of nerve", "funk" and "scrimshanking of the worst type". Lieut-Colonel Viscount Gort of the Grenadier Guards, a much-decorated officer, later to become a Field Marshal, thought that the Regular Army battalions had been comprised of a good class of men, "rather different to those in the New Army units", who were much more likely to go down with shell-shock. Gort did not conceal his low opinion of the type of conscript that was being sent to the BEF later in the war. "The man with fourteen weeks' training," he said, "had not been taught to control himself. He was probably a Yahoo before he was taken into the Army and he could not get his nerves under restraint." Lord Gort was asked by a member of the Committee whether, when Commanding Officers saw that a man was obviously breaking down, they had sent him back to the base. "Yes, but it was a difficulty," he replied. "If you once allowed people to go away you felt you were not playing the game by the Army."[17]

The Committee heard a number of widely-differing opinions on the amount of malingering that had taken place under the pretence of shell-shock. In their Report they dealt with the matter in the following way:

When closely considered, this divergence of views is found to be, to some extent, more apparent than real and the bulk of the evidence is not much at variance. Such discrepancy as exists is partly explicable as arising from the use of the term malingering and as to whether it is interpreted in a limited or broad sense. Again, in those who have been exposed to the stress of battle with its danger, noise and terrors, there is frequent difficulty in deciding how much conscious and how much unconscious motive there may be in the actions of the possible malingerer, since in either case the fundamental instinct of self-preservation is presumably present.[18]

The Committee divided the malingerers into three categories – those who reported sick with feigned shell-shock; those who were really affected with the disorder, but who exaggerated their symptoms in order to prolong their treatment; and the "scrimshankers" who went absent from the line, pleading that they were suffering from shell-shock as an excuse for their delinquency. The numbers in this last group were very large, said the Committee, and if it was right to class them as malingerers, "then it must be allowed that malingering occurred in unprecedented proportions."

Although the Committee investigated the nature, the causes and the treatment of war neurosis in the most extensive manner, their conclusions with regard to shell-shock as a court-martial defence were brief and unsatisfactory. A Major-General who had served as a staff officer in France throughout the war gave evidence that great care had always been taken to prevent shell-shocked soldiers from being condemned to death and executed. If there was the smallest suspicion that a prisoner might have been suffering from war neurosis the sentence was never confirmed by the Commander-in-Chief until the man had been fully examined by an expert in nervous disorders. The Committee accepted the General's assertion without pursuing the matter any further. In their Report they stated that the precautions adopted at courts martial in France seem to have been satisfactory, "namely, that when any medical question or doubt arose before or at a trial, or on subsequent review of the Proceedings, the best possible expert advice available was placed at the immediate disposal of the military authorities, either in the form of a board or otherwise." The

Committee's confidence in the adequacy of these precautions was not diminished, apparently, by other evidence they heard on the point. A doctor who had been a consulting-neurologist in the BEF was of the opinion that a prisoner's state of mind when he had committed an offence in the line could not be ascertained at a subsequent medical examination somewhere in the base area. Equally disquieting was the statement by the senior physician of the Maudsley Neurological Hospital that he would not be prepared to draw a distinction between cowardice and shell-shock. "Cowardice," he said, "I take to mean action under the influence of fear, and the ordinary type of shell-shock to my mind was chronic and persisting fear."[19]

The Committee had considered the proposition that there would have been less shell-shock in the British Army if more attention had been paid to the mental stability of a recruit at his initial medical examination. They were told by the Chief Recruiting Officer for the London District that during the early phases of the war, when floods of volunteers had been enlisting, medical inspections were carried out "in a most haphazard manner". Between 20 and 30 per cent of the recruits never saw a doctor at all, and the remainder had seen one all too briefly; one doctor had examined 400 men every day for ten days. The whole object had been to enlist as many men as possible so that they might be given twelve weeks' training and then rushed out to the trenches. These facts were confirmed by another witness at the Enquiry who had been the Medical Inspector of Recruiting. He added that all through the war many of the men entering the Army had been unfit from a nervous and mental point of view for the stress of active service conditions.[20]

The Committee commented in their Report: "Generally, the evidence we have heard had convinced us that enough attention had not been paid to the mental and psychological aspects of military service."[21]

Several of the witnesses at the Enquiry expressed their doubts as to whether it would have been possible to pick out the new recruits who might break down in action. A senior Major-General said that men of every type of temperament and intelligence were liable to be affected by shell-shock; they had no general characteristics. This opinion was shared by the Director-General of the Army Medical Services who referred to the difficulty of assessing the nervous stability of new recruits at their preliminary examinations. They might appear to a doctor as being timid, highly-strung and lacking in confidence, but nevertheless they might well have the makings of resolute soldiers. The only true test of a man's nerves was his behaviour on the battlefield.[22]

Although the Enquiry was primarily concerned with the Army a few of the witnesses spoke about war neurosis in the other two Services. An Air Vice-Marshal said that cases had been known where pilots of fighter aircraft who had undergone some arduous experience involving a narrow escape from death, for instance by falling out of control from a great height, had been reduced to a state of mental collapse. He had noticed that pilots became more susceptible to shell-shock after they had been in action for a long time and their powers of endurance were exhausted. Some of them relied on alcohol to keep them going.[23]

Among his wartime appointments Dr Rivers had been the Consultant in Psychological Medicine to the Royal Air Force. He informed the Committee that the psycho-neurosis which affected pilots was very slight – "almost trivial compared with the cases seen in the Army." Rivers said he was not surprised by this because man's natural instinct was to escape from a situation of danger, and if he was prevented from doing so he developed stress. When a pilot was engaged in combat his whole attention was concentrated on manoeuvring his plane, whereas the soldier under shellfire in the front line had had to remain inactive in his trench. An air observer was not occupied to the same extent as a pilot and was likely to have a more severe nervous breakdown. Some of the airmen serving in the observation balloon section were the worst cases of the psycho-neurosis Dr Rivers had ever encountered. He attributed this to the fact that for most of the time they were on duty in their balloons they had very little to do and they had known that they were presenting an obvious static target to the enemy.[24]

A submarine commander with the VC said that he had no experience of "shell-shock" in the submarine service; he had only known cases of nerves. He added:

I used to feel an awful funk at times. It is absurd to say you do not. I have yet to meet the fellow who will lie in his ship at the bottom of the sea and be depth-charged and not suffer from cold feet. I felt the strain, but did not realize it at the time. But when you get back to harbour you must have rest. You feel like a washed-out rag. With all these mines around you do not want a depth charge too close to send you to glory.[25]

Chapter 17

Throughout the 1920s there was a great uneasiness among the British public about military executions during the 1914–1918 War, and there had been a growing suspicion that a number of soldiers who were shot for cowardice and desertion might well have been suffering from war neuroses when they had committed the derelictions for which they were condemned. All the papers relating to their courts martial would remain classified documents for seventy-five years after their trials and rumours and speculation abounded. In 1922 an official volume was published entitled *Statistics of the Military Effort of the British Empire during the Great War*.[1] In the section dealing with discipline in the Armed Forces it was disclosed for the first time that a total of 346 men had been sentenced to death and executed, 266 of them for desertion and eighteen for cowardice.

In a Report in 1925 by an Interdepartmental Committee on proposed amendments to the Army and Air Force Act, the members said they could find no foundation for the suggestion that there had been miscarriages of justice at wartime courts martial owing to a failure to distinguish between cowardice and physical breakdown.[2] Their opinion might have carried more weight had it not been for the composition of the Committee. The Chairman was a Conservative Member who had been a Captain in the Royal Navy. The other members were an Admiral, a Lieutenant-General, an Air Vice-Marshal and the legal advisers to the three services.

A short while after the publication of this Report, Ernest Thurtle, a Labour MP, proposed a motion in the House of Commons to exempt certain military offences from the death penalty. During a war, he said, an army was subjected to a very terrible ordeal and if any man was unable to stand up to it – a fault beyond his control – he was liable to be court-martialled and shot. At the conclusion of the debate which followed his speech, the Secretary of State for War announced that the Government could not accept his motion and consequently it was defeated.[3]

At the General Election in 1929 the Labour Party came to power as a minority government. Their first Army and Air Force Bill, introduced in 1930, removed the death penalty for the military offence of cowardice. The new Secretary of State for War explained to the House that the military members of the Army Council still believed that the death penalty was a necessary deterrent which prevented many a man from being a coward, and this was also their opinion with regard to the offence of desertion. Although he had ignored their advice regarding cowardice, he said, he had accepted it in the case of desertion. That was not good enough for Ernest Thurtle, who moved an amendment to the Bill substituting penal servitude for death as the maximum penalty for desertion on active service. The Government allowed a free vote on the amendment and it was carried with a substantial majority.[4]

In spite of a resolute attempt by the House of Lords to restore the death penalty for both cowardice and desertion the Government refused to give way, and the Bill, with Ernest Thurtle's amendment, became law in April, 1930.

The 1914–1918 War was to be "the war to end wars". It seemed unthinkable that the great nations of the world would ever again engage in a conflict which had caused so much slaughter and suffering, so much destruction and havoc.

The League of Nations, designed to make wars impossible in the years to come, was inaugurated at the Paris Peace Conference in 1919. The member states undertook to resolve all future international disputes by arbitration according to the principles of honour and justice; they agreed to a general reduction in armaments, and pledged their governments to the practice of open diplomacy. By the year 1931 fifty-four countries, large and small, including Germany, had joined the League and committed themselves to its objectives.

The Treaty of Versailles, which was settled at the same Paris Peace Conference, imposed the terms of surrender on Germany. The

Rhineland was to be de-militarized and the German frontiers readjusted; the German Army would be restricted to 100,000 officers and men and union between Germany and Austria was expressly forbidden.

The idealistic hopes which had inspired the formation of the League of Nations were shattered in 1933 when Adolf Hitler became Chancellor of Germany and immediately established an absolute dictatorship. His avowed aims were the restoration of the military might of Germany, the recovery – by force if necessary – of the territories which had been ceded under the terms of the Versailles Treaty and the recognition of the Germanic people as the "master-race" of Europe. Before the end of 1933 Germany had withdrawn from the Disarmament Conference and had left the League of Nations. The path was now clear for the fulfilment of Hitler's programme of conquest.

One of the principal objects of the Treaty of Versailles was to prevent the re-emergence of Germany as a military power in the fore-seeable future. Hitler violated with impunity most of the restrictions imposed for this purpose. In March, 1935, he enlarged the German armed forces by the introduction of conscription. In June, 1936, he re-militarized the Rhineland. In February, 1938, he ordered his army to cross the Austrian frontier and incorporated the whole of Austria into Germany. Next, he turned his attention to Czechoslovakia and in September, 1938, by the infamous Munich Agreement, the Czech Government was compelled to evacuate the Sudeten territories and to allow the Germans to take them over. Six months later, in March, 1939, Hitler proclaimed the dissolution of the Czech state and occupied the entire country. So far he had secured all his acquisitions without a shot being fired.

By this time many people in Britain believed that another war against Germany was more or less inevitable. Hitler had wasted no time in pursuing his relentless course of aggression. Having completed the annexation of Czechoslovakia his next intended victim was Poland. As a prelude to invading the country he sought to cut off Polish access to the sea by asserting German sovereignty over the Free City of Danzig. Both France and Britain had undertaken to go to Poland's assistance if she was attacked, and now both nations prepared themselves reluctantly for the approaching conflict. In the spring of 1939 the British Government announced both the doubling of the part-time Territorial Army and the commencement of compulsory military service for all men at the age of 20. Factories started to manufacture more tanks, guns and aircraft; radar defences were extended and increased defensive measures were taken against attack by submarines. At 4.45 a.m. on 1 September, 1939, German troops launched a full-scale attack across the Polish frontier: at 6 a.m. German aircraft bombed Warsaw. Two days later Britain and France declared war on Germany.

In his book *The Face of Battle* John Keegan has said that during the Second World War the psychiatrists in the British Army and, to an even greater extent in the American Army, were able to insist on a proper recognition and treatment of psychiatric cases. He believes this was largely due to the fact that units had been taught how to identify among their recruits both those who were suitable for specialist training and those who were unfitted for any form of military service. Nevertheless, Keegan added, at every stage of the war psychiatric casualties formed a significant percentage of the total casualties in battle.[5]

A psychiatric casualty was officially defined by British Army physicians as "a man who becomes ineffective in battle as a direct result of his personality being unable to stand up to the stresses of combat"[16]. During the Second World War it was found that a number of men who had secret doubts about their own courage developed some form of psychogenic illness – a device of their subconscious minds to avoid the shame of having their cowardice exposed on the battlefield. The most common conditions of this sort were digestive complaints, disordered action of the heart and intractable skin diseases. Thousands of soldiers were discharged from the Army with these ailments before they ever went into action.[7]

As soon as Britain had declared war on Germany an Expeditionary Army began to move to France and before mid-October four Divisions had been moved safely across the Channel. It was a very different situation to that of the BEF in 1914 as they were deployed to the south of Lille along the Franco-Belgian frontier and no British soldiers were in actual contact with the Germans. Their principal role during the autumn and winter months was to strengthen a defensive line by the improvement of a long, continuous anti-tank ditch and the construction of more pill-boxes. Apart from that, they continued their training. Gradually the size of the force was built up and by the end of six months it was composed of ten Divisions. This was a period which became known as "the phoney war", as the vast German and French armies had seemed content to remain immobile in their seemingly impregnable lines. Winston Churchill wrote in his *History of the Second World War*:

> The end of the year 1939 left the war still in its sinister trance. An occasional cannon-shot or reconnoitring patrol alone broke the silence of the Western Front. The armies gaped at each other from behind their rising fortifications across an undisputed "no-man's-land."[8]

Before soldiers go into action, death and physical disability are never far from their minds: few, if any, of them ever envisage the possibility of their becoming psychiatric casualties.

The phoney war ended in the spring of 1940 and the real battle began. On 10 May Hitler invaded Holland and Belgium without warning and opened a general offensive against the French lines. The Allies immediately hurried to the assistance of the Belgians, but for territorial reasons there was little they could do to help the Dutch who were fighting valiantly in the face of tremendous odds. The German attack swept forward relentlessly, spearheaded by powerful armoured and mechanized formations. Their troops were better trained, better armed and better equipped than those of the Allies. Furthermore, they made extensive use of the dive-bomber, which they had first tried out operationally in Poland. This aircraft was designed for both a destructive and a psychological purpose as it emitted a shrill, ear-splitting screech as it hurtled towards the ground in the process of releasing its bombs. It was said that dive-bombers played an important part in the demoralization of the French infantry, particularly of the colonial troops.[9]

On 14 May the small Dutch army abandoned its hopeless struggle and capitulated. The previous day the Germans had broken through the French defences at Sedan. Their tanks and infantry had poured through the gap, encountering little resistance, and had headed for

140

Arras, Amiens and the Channel coast, with the object of encircling the Divisions of the BEF and the ten Divisions of the First French Army, then fighting in Belgium.

On the evening of 20 May advance German formations reached the coast in the area of Abbeville at the mouth of the Somme and encirclement was complete. The position of the BEF was now desperate; it was cut off with dwindling supplies and ammunition. The British War Cabinet and the Chiefs of Staff started at once to draw up emergency plans for evacuating as much of the army as could be saved from the ports of Calais, Boulogne and Dunkirk.

Without pausing, the German armoured and motorized columns struck northwards towards Boulogne and Calais. Boulogne was captured without difficulty and Calais fell a few days later. On 28 May the Belgian Army surrendered, and the BEF, together with the French Divisions fighting by their side, withdrew to a bridgehead around Dunkirk. The evacuation from the port and the beaches had already begun and it was to continue until 4 June. Over 800 vessels took part in the operation – destroyers, pleasure boats, yachts, launches, fishing craft, tugs, lighters and barges. A total of 338,226 troops, including 139,097 Frenchmen, were brought safely back to England.[10] However, they left behind them almost all their tanks, guns and heavy equipment; many soldiers even discarded their rifles before wading from the shore to board the rescue ships.

The entire campaign had only lasted a few weeks, but for the unfledged BEF it had been a harsh initiation to the terrors and the stresses of an innovative form of mobile warfare. They had taken part in an arduous and dispiriting retreat with no lines of communication and with no possibility of reinforcement or relief. Finally, they had endured the strain of intensive shelling and incessant dive-bombing while they were assembled among the sand-dunes waiting for their turn to be taken off from the beaches. And they had been virtually powerless to hit back at the enemy.

It was estimated that out of all the battle casualties sustained by the BEF during the campaign between 10 and 15 per cent were psychiatric.[11] These cases of acute war neuroses were the first the British medical services had encountered since the beginning of the war. After their arrival in England some of the patients were admitted to neurological units straightaway; others had had to spend a few days in general hospitals first. Two psychiatrists, William Sargant and Eliot Slater, who had been working at a special neurological unit in the south of England at the time, described the condition and treatment of some of the men in an article published in *The Lancet* a month after the Dunkirk evacuation.[12] The acute cases of war neurosis in their unit, they said, demonstrated that men of reasonably sound personality might break down if they were subjected to sufficiently severe stress. The soldiers in the BEF had undergone an accumulation of strains, both mental and physical, of great intensity. Apart from actual bodily danger, they had endured constant physical exertion, loss of sleep, insufficient and irregular meals, perpetual bombardment and the sight of their own comrades and unknown civilians being killed all round them. Also, they had been forced to contend with the frustrations of a continual retreat and the impossibility of being able to strike back at their enemy. Later in the war three more psychiatrists, all of whom had treated patients from the BEF during this period, said that additional reasons for their neurotic disturbances had been their repressed feelings of guilt, their resentment at what they believed to be the inadequate leadership they had received and the inferior equipment with which they had had to fight. The men had been reluctant to return to military life because they felt that there would be no security for them anywhere except in the love of their wives or mothers:

> Their army had retreated, their ships were bombed, and their country itself was threatened. They wanted to isolate themselves in small domestic units, but when they did return [home] their neurotic demands could never be gratified; they were dependent children who could not forget the injury done to them. They said, "I am ill and weak and so I cannot serve," but what they meant was, "I can find security only at home and even there no one will protect me from myself."[13]

In their article Sargant and Slater gave a description of the psychiatric casualties when they were first admitted to the neurological unit. The appearance of all the men was remarkably similar, they wrote. Most of them bore the signs of physical exhaustion – thin, fallen-in faces with pallid or sallow complexions. Their expressions and the whole

142

attitude of their bodies indicated either tension and anxiety or a listless apathy. Many had uncontrollable tremors such as those sometimes experienced by patients with Parkinson's disease. Mentally, they were troubled by sleeplessness, terrifying dreams, a feeling of inner unrest and a tendency to be startled by the slightest noise, particularly by the sound of an aeroplane flying overhead or a train passing nearby. Some were affected by amnesia and others by various manifestations of hysteria. One patient underwent a succession of hysterical fits at frequent intervals throughout the day; he would suddenly jump out of bed, throw his hands over his head and give a series of loud groans.[14]

Both Sargant and Slater believed that the physical problems of psychiatric casualties should be dealt with first of all, and that the investigation of their psychological illnesses should not be started until their general health had been restored. The immediate treatment at the unit was uncomplicated: rest, quiet, regular meals and narcotic drugs, especially at nighttime. The milder cases usually improved rapidly. The appearance of the patients became more normal, their tremors decreased and their tension was perceptibly lessened. After a few days in bed they were allowed to get up and were encouraged to engage in some form of occupational therapy. Those who were seriously affected required more care and were sometimes kept on a continuous routine of sedative and hypnotic drugs.[15]

As soon as the patient at the unit was sufficiently recovered physically he was put on a course of psychotherapy. It was essential for him to be able to explain to the doctor the circumstances which had led to his breakdown. Many patients were affected with hysterical amnesia and had no recollection of this vital period. Sometimes their lost memories might return naturally but sometimes they could only be recovered under the influence of hypnosis. It was the task of the physician to discuss with his patient the causes of his neurosis and to try to persuade him to view them in a reasonable and objective way.[16]

Sargant and Slater explained that, since their article had been written so soon after the campaign in France had taken place, they had found it impossible to reach any definite conclusions with regard to the prognosis for the soldiers who had been admitted to their unit. They had both considered it inadvisable to discuss with a patient, during the early stages of his treatment, the prospect of his returning to an active army life. Instead, they had sought to impress on him that

143

he was going to make a complete recovery and that he would presently be restored to his normal state of health. Nevertheless, some of their patients had wanted to talk about their future military service and had expressed a conviction that if they ever went into action again they would break down immediately. Sargant and Slater commented, "If a man firmly believes that he will break down in a particular way in particular circumstances, and he has already done so once, then he will do so again."[17]

The psychiatric casualties from the BEF who were returned to duty after being discharged from hospital were not always completely cured. Lieutenant Leigh, the Regimental Medical Officer at a large driver-training centre of the RASC, to which a number of the ex-patients were sent, kept a careful record of those who were still suffering from psychological illnesses. Five of the men had reported sick within a few weeks, complaining of a general debility. He found that they were affected with tremors, sleeplessness, a rapid pulse-rate and a feeling of physical exhaustion. Two of them had been torpedoed just after being evacuated from Dunkirk and had repeated nightmares about the sinking of their ship. He had diagnosed another five men as having stress dyspepsia brought on by fear and anxiety; this was often accentuated when they were on guard-duty or were under driving instruction. Two men were troubled by effort syndrome, sometimes known as irritable heart, an unusual psychiatric disorder the exact cause of which was unknown. Two others suffered from emotional diarrhoea. They were obsessed with night tremors and frightened by any loud noise. Both had customary neurotic symptoms such as tremors, high pulse rates and persistent insomnia.[18]

For some months after the Dunkirk evacuation the British Army had very few new cases of war neurosis because no British troops were engaged in any active campaign which brought them into close contact with the enemy.

During the summer of 1940 the situation looked exceedingly grim for the Allies. On 11 June the Italian dictator Mussolini, imagining that the fighting was almost finished, entered the war on Hitler's side. On 22 June the French, with their army routed and demoralized, agreed to the terms of a humiliating armistice. The Germans had swept all before them on the continent of Europe and it was expected that they would launch a massive invasion of Britain forthwith. However,

Hitler decided to delay the German landings until the Luftwaffe had pulverized the air defence in the south of England and had broken the spirit of the civil population by the indiscriminate bombing of their cities and their towns. He failed to achieve either of these objectives. The stories of the gallantry of the RAF in the Battle of Britain and the steadfastness of the Londoners during the Blitz have often been recounted. It was a period in the history of the British people which Winston Churchill has described as being "Their Finest Hour".

The next important action in which British troops took part occurred in the Middle East, where the Italians had assembled a large army for an invasion of Egypt. On 6 December, 1940, a mechanized force of about 25,000 British and Australian troops advanced across the Egyptian desert in what had first been intended as a "raid in force", but which had soon developed into a general offensive. After two months fighting the "raiding-party" had seized the whole of Cyrenaica and their forward elements were in the town of Benghazi. Ten Italian Divisions had been destroyed, 1,300 of their guns had been abandoned and 113,000 of their men had been taken prisoner.[19]

During 1941 Britain sustained a succession of serious reverses in the desert and the eastern Mediterranean. At the beginning of the year Hitler had despatched one of his ablest commanders, General Rommel, to Libya in command of the newly-formed Afrika Korps, a German mobile formation specially trained in desert warfare. On 31 March Rommel crossed the borders of Tripolitania and smashed through the British and Australian defensive line. By the middle of April the Afrika Korps were in complete control of Cyrenaica and were poised to drive forward into Egypt. Hitler had invaded Greece early in April in order to assist his hapless ally Mussolini whose army had been striving unsuccessfully to conquer the country since the previous autumn. A small British expeditionary force, consisting of troops from the United Kingdom, Australia and New Zealand, had fought valiantly and briefly alongside the Greeks, but the struggle had been hopeless against the overwhelming strength of the German invaders. After resisting for eight days, Greece had capitulated. Over 50,000 British troops were evacuated from small ports and beaches in the Peloponnese, leaving most of their heavy armament and equipment behind them.[20]

The loss of Greece had made it extremely important for the British to retain control of Crete, which they had occupied at the invitation of the Greek Government. The RAF had been making extensive use of the airfields on the island and the Royal Navy had established a fuelling base in the port at Suda Bay. The War Cabinet in London had issued orders that Crete must be held at all costs, both for the preservation of Britain's dominance in the eastern Mediterranean and for its strategical value in the defence of Egypt. However, the men and materials had not been sufficient for the task. The German invasion had begun on 20 May with the largest airborne landing that had ever taken place in warfare and the garrison had only been able to hold out for little more than a week. Once again there was a hurried and hazardous evacuation, and once again it had been successfully carried out by the Royal Navy. Over 16,000 troops were taken off and carried safely to Egypt; about 5,000 of their comrades, who were still fighting, had been authorized to surrender to the enemy.[21]

After the battle of Crete and before the end of 1941 two momentous events occurred which had completely changed the face of the war. The first of these happened on 22 June, when Hitler attacked Soviet Russia and German armies surged across the Russian frontiers from the Baltic to the Black Sea. The second took place on 7 December, when the Japanese, without any prior warning, carried out a heavy air raid on the United States Naval Base at Pearl Harbor and crippled the American Pacific Fleet. From then on Britain and the nations of the Commonwealth no longer stood alone.

Chapter 18

In mid-December, 1941, Winston Churchill and his Chiefs of Staff visited Washington for a discussion on future strategy. It was feared by the British that, in consequence of the attack at Pearl Harbor, the Americans might regard the Japanese as their principal enemies and look upon the war against Hitler as a secondary consideration. In fact, it was made clear at the outset that this was not the case: the immediate purpose of the United States would be to bring about the defeat of Nazi Germany.[1] It was agreed at the Washington talks that victory over the Germans could only be achieved by an Anglo-American invasion of the mainland of Europe and that such an operation could not possibly be mounted before 1943. The main objective for the campaign of 1942 was to be a landing in French North Africa and the occupation of the Mediterranean coastline by British and American forces.[2]

For many years it had been the almost universal view of both civil and military psychiatrists in the United States that men with predisposing character and personality defects would be particularly vulnerable to the stresses of the battlefield and that war neurosis in the Army could be largely eliminated if mentally unsuitable recruits were prevented from enlisting.[3] A special directive had been issued to all local recruitment boards by the Selective Service Headquarters on 15 December, 1941, stating that examining physicians should have far more information regarding a man's medical and social background when assessing whether or not he was fit for service in the armed forces. It seems that this had very little effect, and during the massive expansion of the American Army

147

immediately after Pearl Harbor the neuro-psychiatric examination of recruits at most of the induction centres was cursory, often lasting only for a couple of minutes. At some centres about 200 men were examined by a single psychiatrist every day. The hurried interviews, said the medical historian Albert Deutsch, were "little more than a farce, in which the hapless psychiatrist had to spice his knowledge and experiences with hunches and fortune telling". Deutsch believed that as many as 50 per cent of the psychiatric casualties in the American Army could have been avoided if the social histories of the recruits had been obtainable at their initial examinations.[4] Nevertheless, between January, 1942, and May, 1943, out of every hundred men examined at induction centres throughout the United States an average of seven or eight were rejected for neuro-psychiatric reasons. They comprised about a third of the total number of men who were rejected for any causes, physical or mental.[5]

After the Armistice in 1918 the medical section of the United States Army had been reorganized and the neuro-psychiatric branch in the Surgeon General's office was disbanded. During the early months of 1943 there had been a great deal of indecision among the American higher commanders in regard to the establishment of an efficient system for the segregation and treatment of soldiers affected with war neurosis. It was partly due to the insistence of the American Psychiatric Association that a senior medical officer, Colonel Roy Halloran, was appointed to make arrangements for the reception and care of psychiatric casualties. Halloran could appreciate the problems which would be involved as he had served under Dr Thomas Salmon during the First World War. He immediately contacted the headquarters of the Royal Army Medical Corps in London to find out the most recent experience in the British campaigns of the past two years and he arranged for special schools to be set up where regimental doctors could be taught how to deal with the cases of war neurosis they would come across in battle. It was soon possible for a psychiatrist to be assigned to the headquarters of every United States combat division.[6]

At this stage of the war the incidence of war neurosis in the British Army was inconsiderable as most of the troops were still based in the UK, both to meet the continuing threat of a German invasion and to train for an eventual landing on the European mainland. A.J.P. Taylor has written:

> The fighting men were much more part of the community and much less a race apart than they had been in the First World War. A great many of them were stationed in Great Britain – a large part of navy and the air force all along, and then the army accumulating for the invasion of France; while on the other side civilians in the Home Guard, civil defence, or merely being bombed, were clearly in the war.[7]

In the Far East a force of British and Dominion troops, ill-prepared and irresolute, was engaged in a hopeless struggle against a highly-trained Japanese army, which overran the whole of the Malayan peninsula and captured Singapore with its 85,000 defenders. Hong Kong had also surrendered with its complete garrison. Japan was not a signatory of the Geneva Convention and the prisoners of war were treated with the utmost brutality.

Britain had encountered other adversities in 1942. Tobruk had fallen to the Afrika Korps in June and the way was opened for Rommel to attack Alexandria. In August an ill-fated raid was mounted on the Channel port of Dieppe. Most of the landing force, comprised of Canadians and British Commandos, failed to get clear of the beaches and the attack had to be abandoned. More than half of the Canadian troops who had taken part were either killed or taken prisoner. It was said that Dieppe, in spite of the grim casualty figures, provided some valuable lessons which greatly assisted the Allies in the planning of further opposed landings[8]

In the autumn of 1942 the tide of battle swung in favour of the Allies. At the end of October the British Desert Army, then commanded by the redoubtable General Sir Bernard Montgomery, went into the attack with three armoured and the equivalent of seven infantry Divisions. After twelve days of hard fighting they inflicted a severe defeat on the German and Italian forces under the command of General Rommel. The enemy were swept back in a fifteen-hundred-mile retreat which forced Rommel to abandon the whole of Cyrenaica and Tripoli.

During the early hours of the morning on 8 November, 1942,

American and British troops had started to land on the coasts of Algeria and Morocco. It was hoped that the North African campaign could be finished fairly rapidly, but it had lasted far longer than was expected. The unloading of ships had been hampered by constant air attacks on the ports; the movement of supplies was restricted by the scarcity and the poor quality of the roads; and, above all, General Rommel, now in overall command of the recently strengthened German and Italian forces in North Africa, had retreated into Tunis where he had established strong defensive positions.

It was not until 13 May, 1943, that victory was finally won, and General Alexander, the Deputy Commander of the Allied armies, had been able to signal Winston Churchill:

> Sir,
>   It is my duty to report that the Tunisian campaign is over. All enemy resistance has ceased. We are masters of the North African shores.[9]

The British Divisions in the field were growing accustomed to psychiatric casualties, which were far more common in static than in mobile types of fighting. Regimental officers and NCOs in infantry battalions had learnt to recognize the symptoms in the early stages of the disorder. The man became scruffy and unkempt in appearance, he neglected to care for his personal weapon and he neither washed nor shaved until he was ordered to do so. Later he developed a tremor in his hands and a terrified, hunted look came to his eyes. This was known in the army as "going bomb-happy". Other men, after a long spell in action, suddenly broke down in uncontrollable tears or became indolent and apathetic.[10] It was customary to send back bomb-happy soldiers to the rear as soon as possible. They had become totally ineffective, a burden to their comrades and a source of demoralization.

It has been estimated that in the various actions fought by the British Army during the Second World War, depending on the type of fighting, from 2 per cent to 30 per cent of all battle casualties were psychiatric. In the desert campaign during the middle of 1942 the figure was between 7 and 10 per cent.[11]

It was the accepted medical opinion that the recovery of psychiatric

150

casualties was more rapid and more lasting if they were treated close to the front line and were returned to duty as quickly as possible.[12] It was also the view that it should be impressed upon the patients from the outset of their treatment that their condition was only temporary and that they were suffering from no actual or physical illness.[13] After a period of prolonged rest, induced by sedative drugs, good food and reassurance, approximately 70 to 80 per cent of them were able to go back to their units.[14] The worst cases had to be evacuated to hospitals at the base.[15]

The United States Army, like the British, sustained a high proportion of psychiatric casualties during the Second World War. The expeditionary force which had landed in North Africa was largely composed of troops who had never been in action before and the majority of the enlisted men were very young. During the previous autumn Congress had lowered the minimum draft age from 20 to 18, despite the opposition of some members of the medical and teaching professions who argued that youths of 18 and 20 would be too immature to face the rigours of the battlefield.[16] General George Marshall, the American Chief of Staff, complained in 1943 that the number of soldiers being discharged from the army on psychiatric grounds was greater than the number being inducted.[17] During the Tunisia campaign about a third of the American battle casualties were psychiatric.[18]

In an effort to remove the last remaining vestiges of stigma from war neurosis, the United States Army adopted the diagnostic terms of "battle-fatigue" and "combat exhaustion" to describe the disorder.[19] An official American report on psychiatric casualties stated:

> There is no such thing as "getting used to combat". . . . Each moment of combat imposes a strain so great that men will break down in direct relation to the intensity and duration of their exposure . . . psychiatric casualties are as inevitable as gunshot and shrapnel wounds in modern warfare. . . . Most men were ineffective after 180, or even 140 days. The general consensus was that a man reached the peak of his effectiveness in the first 90 days of combat, that after that his efficiency began to fall off, and that he became steadily less valuable thereafter until he was utterly useless. The number of men on

151

duty after 200 to 240 days of combat was small and their value to their units was negligible.[20]

In the United States Army, as in the British, it was considered that the majority of the psychiatric casualties should be treated close to the front, as it was believed that the further the patients were removed from the places where they had broken down the less likely it became that they would recover sufficiently to return to duty. Only the more severe cases were evacuated to base hospitals. The customary treatment was relaxation and tranquillization. Intensive use was made of barbiturate drugs.[21] Just over 60 per cent of the men were able to go back to their units in the line.[22]

Two American medical officers have described the condition of some of the soldiers suffering from severe war neurosis during the Tunisian campaign. These patients, they said, presented an intensely striking and unforgettable picture on first being admitted to hospital. They were terror-stricken, mute and tremulous.

> Their facial expression may be vacuous or fearful and apprehensive. Speech is usually impossible except for a few stuttering attempts to frame an occasional word; nevertheless, patients persist in attempting to communicate with the attendants and some may be able to write, although unable to talk. Sudden fits of crying or laughing may result without reason. Behaviour is extremely bizarre with senseless gestures and alternating periods of excessive activity, characterized by running about the ward and leaping over beds.[23]

Any sudden, loud noise caused the patient to react in a startled manner, the Medical Officers continued. He jumped, trembled violently and turned his head in the direction of the sound with an expression of fear on his face. "Terror is the principal theme of the patient's behaviour," they said. "He resembles a frightened, inarticulate child."[24]

It was the experience of the two Medical Officers that mild cases of combat exhaustion recovered fairly rapidly with adequate rest, warmth and good food. During their treatment the patients continued to suffer from insomnia and nightmares, and they were perpetually

152

worried by the notion that they had failed in their duty by showing a lack of courage. The Medical Officers had encountered very few instances of malingering. It was difficult, they said, for war neurosis to be malingered, even superficially, because any pretence of the condition would soon be revealed.[25]

It was decided by the Allied Chiefs-of-Staff that the main invasion of the European mainland would have to be postponed until 1944 and that in the meanwhile a landing would take place in Italy. This was partially to keep up the momentum of the attack on the Axis powers and partially to divert as many German troops as possible from the Russian front. Sicily was to be occupied first in order to clear the sea-route and to capture the Sicilian airfields before the land-attack on Italy was commenced.

The invasion of Sicily by the Americans and the British took place on 10 July. It was by no means an easy operation as the island was defended by more than 400,000 German and Italian soldiers, and was heavily fortified. After the enemy had recovered from their initial surprise at the landings they put up a stubborn resistance, but the whole of Sicily was in the hands of the Allies by 17 August.

Meanwhile, events had taken a dramatic turn in Italy. On 25 July the discredited dictator Mussolini was deposed and interned. A new Italian government headed by the veteran army officer Marshal Badoglio immediately approached the Allies with a view to settling the terms of an armistice. Italy officially surrendered on 3 September, the day when British and Canadian troops crossed the narrow Straits of Messina from Sicily, to land near the town of Reggio on the southern tip of the Italian mainland. A week later an Anglo-American landing took place at Salerno, higher up the west coast towards Naples.

On 12 September ninety German paratroops rescued Mussolini from his confinement in a small mountain resort in central Italy and flew him to Germany. As a result he set up a puppet Fascist government in the north of the country and Italy became embroiled in a civil war. Until then it had seemed that the whole country might be taken by the Allies without too much trouble. Now the situation had changed. The Germans had decided to end their retreat and to hold a defensive line to the south of Rome, where the features of the terrain formed a natural obstacle to the progress of an advancing army. With the approach of winter and the deteriorating weather conditions the British and American troops became committed to what General Eisenhower, the Supreme Commander of the Allied forces, described as being "a long and costly slogging match" against an enemy who was able to relieve his formations at the front without much difficult.[26] Severe fighting continued throughout the winter and the following spring. Rome was not captured by the Allies until early in June, 1944.

During the winter months the incidence of psychopathic disorders among both the British and American forces in Italy had been very high. In fact, in one spell of forty-four days' continuous fighting 54 per cent of all the casualties sustained by the American 2nd Armoured Division had been psychiatric.[27] The rate of desertions from the British Divisions had also been high and at one time the senior commanders had pressed the War Office to make the offence punishable by execution.[28] The American Army adopted a more understanding attitude to the effects of battle-strain and the United States court-martial manual directed that, when an accused soldier might have been mentally disturbed at the time of his offence, he should be referred to a psychiatrist for examination before he was sentenced.[29]

On 6 June, 1944, known thereafter as D-Day, a combined American, British and Canadian force took part in the greatest amphibious operation ever mounted. By nightfall more than 156,000 men had been landed on the coast of Normandy. Hitler had boasted that what he called the "Atlantic Wall" was impregnable and he had allocated sixty Divisions under one of his most experienced commanders, Field Marshal von Rundstedt, to defend it. A week after D-Day Stalin had sent a telegram to Churchill congratulating him on the Allied achievement. "My colleagues and I cannot but admit," he said, "that the history of warfare knows no other like undertaking from the point of view of its scale, its vast conception, and in its masterly execution."[30]

During the weeks which followed the landings the invasion forces made little progress as they found it impossible to break out from the narrow confines of the bridgehead. The Bocage, which covers most of Normandy, consists of a series of small fields surrounded by ditches, banks and very thick hedgerows which could be almost as impenetrable as barbed-wire barricades. For troops to advance across such country against an enemy in well-prepared positions was both extremely difficult and extremely costly. When an infantry battalion was carrying out an attack, the forward companies frequently lost a third of their men in killed and wounded.[31] To add to the difficulties of the invaders the worst storm for forty years blew up in the Channel in the middle of June. For four days the gale raged, completely destroying one of the two artificial harbours upon which they were relying for their reinforcements and material and severely damaging the other. The gunners were just about to run out of shells when the winds died down.

Eventually, on 25 July, the Americans succeeded in breaking through the cordon at St Lô, to the south of the Cherbourg peninsula, and the whole of the Allied Force was able to move forward from the bridgehead. Hitler, ignoring the advice of his Generals, had ordered his army to launch a mammoth counter-attack. It ended in total failure and in the virtual annihilation of eight of Field Marshal von Rundstedt's most dependable Divisions. The Allies, by then, were driving back the Germans in headlong retreat in every sector of the Front and the Battle of Normandy was over.

It had been realized that the stresses of the Normandy invasion would result in an appreciable number of psychiatric casualties and special wards were set aside for their reception at various English hospitals.

A few weeks after D-Day, in an article in *The Lancet*, three psychiatrists described the condition of some of the patients at their hospital who had broken down during the initial ten days of fighting after the landing.[32] They said that all these men had been serving in combatant units – the commandos, the assault infantry or the airborne regiment. Their ages varied between 18 and 32; their average length of service was about three and a half years; 80 per cent of them had not been in action before and 20 per cent had fought in Africa, Sicily or Italy. They had all been admitted to hospital with the provisional diagnosis that they were suffering from "combat exhaustion". The three psychiatrists criticized this classification on the ground that none of the patients had been exhausted at the time of their admission. Further, some of the more neurotic cases, knowing the medical name for their condition, had convinced themselves that they were too

155

exhausted to leave their stretchers and that they would remain enfeebled for the rest of their lives.

On their arrival at the hospital 12 per cent of the men had been unable to speak, 8 per cent were temporarily blind, 7 per cent had lost their hearing and 15 per cent had developed a stammer. None of them was affected by paralysis. Of the lesser neurotic symptoms, some had tremors, some were affected by fits of weeping and some were startled by every sudden noise. As many as 70 per cent had habitual nightmares relating to their battle experiences. In contrast to the war-neurotic patients after the Dunkirk evacuation four years before, said the psychiatrists, these men had a high morale and were reluctant to discuss their emotional and physical discomforts. They had confidence in their leaders and they trusted their weaponry. The majority were not worried by a sense of shame because they had broken down, but believed that their comrades would accept that they had succumbed to a temporary indisposition for which they needed rest and sleep.

The psychiatrists who wrote the article paid tribute to the regimental medical officers who had dealt with the psychiatric casualties soon after they had broken down and had prevented an early form of neurosis from developing into a more serious psychological disorder. As a consequence of the prompt and effective care which they had received at the Front the majority of the patients had considerably improved by the time they reached the hospital and required no more medication for the neurotic disorder, although a few of them were still in need of sedation and were kept on narcotic drugs for another few days. As a general rule, after a short time in bed, the patients were made to get up and to take part in such activities as physical training and occupational therapy. They were encouraged to talk freely about their battle experiences and to recount their nightmares.

During the first ten days' fighting after the landing in Normandy more than 10 per cent of the British battle casualties were psychiatric. In the struggle to break out of the bridgehead the figure increased to 20 per cent.[33]

As a result of the successful D-Day invasion the scale of the battle expanded rapidly and more and more units of the British Army became involved in the fighting. This led to a significant increase in the number of soldiers affected by war neurosis. After the breakout

156

from the bridgehead forward medical centres were set up in France in which psychiatric casualties could receive treatment and only the severe cases were sent back to one of the special hospitals in England. The largest of these was Hollymoor Hospital in Birmingham which had been taken over by the military in April, 1942. Patients usually remained there for six to eight weeks.[34]

It was hoped that after leaving Hollymoor most of the ex-patients would be able to return to the Army for non-combatant duties. The principal contribution the hospital made to the treatment of war neurosis was the innovation of a system of psychological rehabilitation by regular periods of group therapy. Because close relationships were enforced by military life, the doctors believed that the curative process for the men's disorders would be more beneficial if it was carried out collectively. Not all the healing methods practised at Hollymoor were so conventional. For instance, there was a procedure known as "compulsory mourning". Sometimes a patient who had been a tank commander had had a nervous breakdown because members of his crew had been killed so often that he had lost the ability to be saddened by their deaths. If this was the cause of his disorder, the hospital confined him alone in a darkened room for three days and ordered him to spend the time grieving for his dead comrades. During the period of detainment he was only allowed two hours of light and he was kept on a diet of bread and water. It was claimed at the hospital that these draconian measures proved successful in curing this type of neurosis.[35]

The methods used for the disposal and treatment of psychiatric casualties in the American forces were very similar to those employed by the British. The men were admitted to forward medical centres, positioned close to the front line, where they were given tranquillizing drugs and encouraged to rest. When they were sufficiently stable they took part in sessions of psychotherapy. The majority were returned to duty as quickly as possible and only the worst cases were evacuated to hospitals in England or the United States.[36]

During the whole of the Second World War 409,887 members of the American Armed Forces were admitted as neuro-psychiatric patients to military hospitals overseas. Of these, 127,000 men were returned to the United States. It has been estimated that about 23 per cent of the American soldiers evacuated from combat areas for medical reasons were psychiatric casualties.[37]

At an early stage in the war it was recognized by the Royal Air Force that flying personnel, especially aircrews in Bomber Command, were subject to psychological disorders, and special centres were set up at which they could be classified and treated. Most of their neuroses were similar to those affecting soldiers on active service. An airman who broke down while engaged in combat flying was said to be suffering from "Lack of Moral Fibre".

A report on aircrew psychiatric casualties in RAF hospitals during the war stated that the main cause of the illness was fear.

> Most of the patients were very much afraid, and their fear was most intense when in the air. Either the fear itself, or the conflict which arose between their intense fear and their accepted standard of behaviour, appears to have been the precipitating factor in causing the psychological disorder in most cases.[38]

During the year 1942–1943 a total of 2,989 airmen were adjudged to be suffering from Lack of Moral Fibre. Of these 35.1 per cent were able to resume full flying duty and 7.1 per cent limited flying duty. Of the remainder 55.9 per cent were grounded and 1.8 per cent were invalided out of the service. For the year 1943–1944 the number said to lack moral fibre went up to 3,296 and only 37.6 per cent recovered sufficiently to resume either full or limited flying duty. Of the rest, 60.2 per cent were grounded and 2.1 per cent were invalided out.[39]

According to the Report, when a squadron lost a lot of planes on operations it was apt to cause a panic among the remaining aircrews, who started to speculate about their own chances of survival. This had a very bad effect on morale.[40]

A survey was carried out during the war in which 300 members of aircrews in Bomber Command were asked individually which hazards they feared most when they were engaged in operational flying. The men selected for the survey had all been on a minimum of ten missions over Germany and none of them had ever suffered from any psychological disorders. The majority said that fog was their principal concern as it gave them a feeling of helplessness and apprehension. Next, they dreaded their plane being hit by anti-aircraft fire or being trapped in the glare of enemy searchlights. They also had a horror of being disfigured by burns. No one who was questioned was ashamed of being afraid, as long as he could hide it from the others in his crew. All the men were agreed that fear was a natural emotion for aircrews during operational flying and that the last few sorties on a tour of duty became progressively more and more frightening.[41]

It was known that the aircrews of bomber planes occasionally took off on a mission, but turned back long before they had reached the target area, sometimes reporting a fictitious defect in their aircraft. A Flight Sergeant whose plane had returned prematurely from a bombing raid on Germany in 1944 recounted the incident on a television programme years later. He had broken down on the outward flight while they were still over England. He had worked himself up to such a state of terror, he said, that he actually froze with fear and he was unable to speak or move. The rest of his crew had decided to abandon the mission and to return to their aerodrome because of his condition. Afterwards he was seen by his Commanding Officer who told him he could either resume his aircrew duties or he could decline to fly again and be branded as a coward for the rest of his life. He had chosen to ignore his breakdown and to carry on in his squadron.[42]

Before a candidate was accepted for aircrew training in the American Air Force he had to undergo an elaborate series of psychological tests, lasting for about ten hours, to ensure that he had the required emotional and temperamental stability. Air Force personnel who suffered from what was known as "flyers' fatigue" or "fatigue syndrome" were sent for treatment to rest camps well away from the battle area.[43]

In 1943 two American Medical Officers, both serving in Tunis, were requested by the Surgeon General of the Army Air Forces to write a report on the principal war neuroses sustained by flying personnel during the fighting in North Africa. Their report was later circulated to all American Air Force stations. They stated that depression was common among crews of bomber aircraft. It was sometimes caused by the death of a close friend in their squadron and sometimes by their surviving a crash in which others had been killed. The Medical Officers said that they knew of one case in which a pilot had been so convinced of his own responsibility for crashing his plane that he was afraid to fly again in case he had another crash and killed more members of his crew.[44]

In their Report the Medical Officers said that some members of aircrews were obsessed by the belief that they could not survive many more bombing missions. They frequently turned to alcohol for relief from their depression and sometimes drank to excess before their neuroses were recognized.[45]

Germany surrendered unconditionally to the Allies on 7 May, 1945. Japan fought on for another few months and surrendered on 14 August.

Chapter 19

During the years immediately after 1945 ex-servicemen suffering from war neurosis were much less in evidence than the shell-shock victims had been in the period following the First World War. The main reason for this was that they were far fewer in number: also, there were greater facilities for their employment and welfare. Nevertheless, many of them ended up in homes or under constant care. Typical examples were three of the cases in one of the Treatment Centres run by Combat Stress, the Ex-Services Mental Welfare Society. The first was an infantryman who had taken part in the fighting in the Normandy bridgehead where his battalion had sustained more than 90 per cent casualties. Years later he was still suffering from severe depression, bouts of crying, panic attacks and nightmares. The second had been an ambulance driver in North Africa. He was deeply affected by the dead bodies he had had to collect from the battlefields and the badly-wounded for whom so little could be done until they reached a hospital. Afterwards he had been plagued by nightmares and feelings of guilt because of his inability to ease the pain of many of the wounded men. When his memories overwhelmed him he would shut himself into a room alone and break down in tears. The third patient had been a sergeant and had been wounded during the attempted relief of Arnhem. Ever since he was demobilized at the end of the war he had been troubled by perpetual nightmares relating to the occasion on which he was wounded and by an immutable belief that, as a senior NCO, he might have been responsible for the deaths of some of his men.[1]

It was found that war neurosis was a condition which could remain dormant for a long time, and then could develop very suddenly. The publicized commemorations of wartime battles sometimes caused the emergence of psychoneurotic symptoms among the veterans who had actually taken part in them. During the two months after the celebration of the fiftieth anniversary of the D-Day landing in Normandy more than a thousand ex-servicemen contacted Combat Stress to seek their assistance.[2]

An interesting study of the long-term effects of battle experiences on young men was conducted in the United States after the Second World War by the psychiatrist Dr George Valliant. The subjects of the study were 152 ex-soldiers who had all been students at Harvard University between 1939 and 1944 and had joined the Army at an average age of 22. On their return to civilian life in 1946 it was found that seventeen of the group had symptoms of war neurosis: one, who was more seriously affected, later committed suicide. In 1995 those of the subjects of the study who were alive were re-assessed. Most of the men who had had combat-related symptoms in 1946 reported that their condition had neither worsened nor improved during the intervening years, but it had neither interfered with their work nor their social existence. None of the other surviving members of the group had developed any new manifestations which could definitely be associated with war neurosis.[3]

Dr Simon Wessely, a consultant psychiatrist, writing in *The Times* about the Harvard investigation said:

> What this exceptional study has shown is that psychological reactions to trauma, if they occur, persist. The worse the trauma, the more the symptoms. The normal processes by which we adapt to psychological distress do not seem to happen with such intense experiences . . . memories of wartime combat do not fade away.[4]

After the end of the Second World War the next major military action fought by the United States of America was the Korean campaign, in which Britain also took part. In 1945 it had been agreed by the Allies that Soviet Russia would accept the Japanese surrender close to the 38th parallel in Korea. Thereafter, a Communist state, supported by the Russians, had been established in the northern part of the Korean peninsula, whilst a pro-western régime, supported by the United

States of America, had come into being in the southern part. Various attempts were made to unify the country, but they all failed and the two governments had become more and more polarized in their respective ideologies. By 1949 most of the Russian and American troops had been withdrawn completely from both parts of Korea.

On 25 June, 1950, the North Koreans, with the approval of the Soviet Union, crossed the 38th parallel and invaded the southern part of the country. Their army, trained and equipped by the Russians, brushed aside the inferior South Korean forces and advanced rapidly down the peninsula. The United Nations Security Council met immediately in emergency session and passed a Resolution calling on all its members to send military contingents to Korea, under UN auspices, to resist the North Korean aggression. The United States reacted swiftly and very soon four American Divisions were fighting alongside the South Koreans.

Even with the help of the Americans, the South Korean army was no match for the invaders and almost the whole of the peninsula had been overrun when, on 15 September, 1950, troops under General Douglas MacArthur carried out a daring amphibious landing in the rear of the North Korean line, cutting off most of their forward troops. The American and South Korean forces then fought their way back to the 38th parallel. They were warned by the Chinese that if they advanced any further the presence of their soldiers would constitute a threat to the security of China. In spite of this threat, MacArthur continued to drive into North Korea with the intention of setting up a single government for the whole country. A short while later China entered the war and approximately 180,000 Chinese "volunteers", who were in reality professional soldiers, went into action against the U.N. forces.

The Korean conflict then developed into a full-scale war. The UN Army, commanded by General MacArthur, consisted mainly of South Koreans and Americans but also included contingents from Britain, Australia, New Zealand, Turkey and Ethiopia. On the Communist side there were North Koreans and eventually over a million Chinese. The Russians gave unstinting military support to the North Koreans but never actually committed their troops to the fighting.

The struggle continued for the whole of 1951 and 1952 with neither army gaining a clear advantage. After months of indecisive

163

negotiations an armistice was finally concluded in July, 1953, which left Korea still divided into two separate and hostile states. It was estimated that there had been more than 4,000,000 casualties during the three years of the Korean War, most of whom had been civilians. A total of 33,629 American soldiers had been killed.

Directly American troops became involved in the Korean campaign arrangements were initiated by the army medical services for dealing with cases of war neurosis. The psychiatric screening procedure, which had proved to be a failure during the Second World War, was abandoned. Battalion aid stations were established for units in the front line, as well as forward treatment centres at the divisional level. The diagnosis of "exhaustion" in these cases was altered to "combat exhaustion" to indicate that the patient was suffering from a psychiatric breakdown rather than from physical prostration. The term "combat fatigue" was also used.[5]

During the period from July, 1950, until December, 1952, approximately 37 American soldiers out of every 1000 who were serving in Korea were treated in Divisional or Base psychiatric hospitals each year. The lowest annual rate for the American Army in the Second World War had been 28 men per 1000, and the highest rate 101 per 1000. It was estimated from the medical statistics of the American Expeditionary Force in France that no soldier could remain in action for more than 180 days without becoming a psychiatric casualty. In an effort to reduce the number of men who broke down under the stress of battle, the American forces in Korea employed a rotation system by which every soldier serving in the line was relieved individually at regular intervals. In addition, no soldier was expected to serve in the Korean campaign for longer than a maximum of nine months.[6]

The methods of treating psychiatric casualties in the field which had been developed during the Second World War were continued in Korea. The forward psychiatric centres were situated as close to the combat area as possible, and directly a patient had been rested and cured of the manifestations of his illness he was sent back to his unit. In the view of the military psychiatrists the soldier succumbed to combat exhaustion or combat fatigue simply because he had failed, temporarily or more persisently, to confront the conditions of battle. During the whole of the campaign only 6 percent of the psychiatric casualties had to be evacuated from Korea.[7]

164

The next major military involvement of the United States Army had been in Vietnam. Lord Rees-Mogg, the former Editor of *The Times*, has said that "The Vietnam War did to America what the Somme did for Britain; it destroyed the confidence of the public in the competence of the elite, and destroyed the confidence of the elite in itself."[8]

Indochina had become a French colonial possession in the 19th century and had remained so until it was occupied by the Japanese during the Second World War. At the Potsdam Conference of the victorious Allies in 1945 it was agreed that the French should take over Indochina once more. The presence of a colonial power was not accepted by the Communist-led Viet Minh faction which immediately began a guerrilla campaign of armed resistance. After a short struggle the French granted Viet Minh a semi-autonomous free state, Vietnam, within the French Union. However, the Viet Minh would be satisfied with nothing less than total independence, and encouraged by the Communist government of China, they continued their guerrilla operations on an ever-mounting scale. By the middle of 1953 they were in control of most of the country and the French, accepting the inevitable, negotiated a cease-fire at an international conference in Geneva.

By the terms of the Geneva Agreement the country was to be divided into two separate military zones at the 17th parallel, the Communists having the part to the north of the line and the non-communists that to the south. The result was predictable. The northern zone, now called the Democratic Republic of Vietnam, became an outpost of the communist empire, its armed forces trained and equipped by China and Soviet Russia, while the United States began to provide military supplies and advisors to the South. War broke out between the two states in 1960.

Early in 1965 American warships patrolling off the coast of North Vietnam were attacked by torpedo boats. President Lyndon Johnson instantly authorized retaliatory air-strikes against North Vietnamese naval bases, and Congress approved a resolution ordering "all necessary measures" to be taken in order to protect American forces from any further attacks. This marked the start of the Americanization of the Vietnam War. Within a few months 75,000 American troops were taking part in the campaign, fighting at the side of some 600,000 South Vietnamese.

Three years after the United States became involved in the war over half a million American soldiers were serving in Vietnam. In spite of the enormous quantities of modern military equipment they had at their disposal, and the fact that North Vietnam was subjected to continual, intensive bombing by the American air force, their efforts were singularly unsuccessful against an enemy who relied very largely on guerrilla tactics and underground warfare.

As American casualties mounted, the campaign in Vietnam became increasingly unpopular in the United States and there was a growing conviction among the politicians in Washington that military victory for either side would be an impossibility. When Richard Nixon was elected President in 1968 he ordered a restriction of the bombing of North Vietnam and began negotiations with the North Vietnamese government. The new President also started to withdraw American troops and return them to the United States, but others remained in the combat areas for several years more until a cease-fire agreement was concluded in January, 1973. By then nearly 58,000 Americans had been killed or were still missing. Three million Vietnamese had perished during the war.[9]

At the time the United States became embroiled in Vietnam the American Army was fully prepared for the handling of large numbers of psychiatric casualties. In previous years it had been emphasized in military training schools and on staff courses that there would always be soldiers who broke down in battle and that they needed to be dealt with by properly qualified medical officers at divisional level. An American Division had a numerical strength of between 15,000 and 18,000 men. Every combat Division in Vietnam had on its establishment a psychiatrist, a social worker and eight mental hygiene specialists.[10]

In fact, the psychiatric breakdown rate among American troops in Vietnam was considerably lower than had been expected and was less than that of American forces in either the Second World War or in Korea. Several different reasons have been suggested for the decrease. The rotation system was applied by the American High Command from the start and no man was allowed to serve in a combat area for more than a total of 365 days. This stipulation created extreme difficulties in the administration of the army as a constant check had to be kept on each individual soldier to ensure that he did not exceed the limit of the time he was permitted to be on active service. It also meant that men were constantly joining and leaving their units, which hampered the development of true comradeship and mutual trust.[11] Another factor which may have contributed to the decline of the incidence of war neurosis was the fact that the Vietnam war was a "low intensity" campaign. The battle zones remained comparatively fluid and soldiers did not have to spend long periods in trenches or foxholes; in addition, they were very rarely subjected to artillery barrages or aerial bombing. To offset this there was the significant psychological determinant that the war had never been popular either with the troops in the field or with the general public in the United States. After serving for a few months in Vietnam most soldiers were overcome by feelings of frustration and helplessness and they had been aware that, when they returned home after completing their tours of duty, they would not be treated as heroes, nor even as men who had just fulfilled a patriotic obligation.[12]

American troops in Vietnam passed through a period of maximum vulnerability to war neurosis during their first three months in a combat zone. After that they became less prone to the disorder. Throughout the campaign the annual incidence rate for psychiatric casualties had varied between ten and twelve men for every 1000 who were in contact with the enemy. These soldiers were usually treated at Divisional or Base centres and only the patients needing more than thirty days in hospital were evacuated from the battle area. The treatment for war neurosis was much the same as it had been in the Korean War, except for the advent of several new tranquillizing drugs.[13]

Although the number of American psychiatric casualties in Vietnam was lower than had been anticipated, a large proportion of the veterans suffered from symptoms of war neurosis during the ensuing years after the cease-fire. It has been suggested that the memories of the campaign were particularly stressful for them because of the general unpopularity of the war, the lack of moral justification for it, the rumours of atrocities committed by their own troops, the protracted and indecisive nature of the struggle and their widespread drug abuse in an effort to sustain morale.[14]

Immediately after the end of the Vietnam War a new diagnostic description came into being for the psychiatric illnesses which were suffered by the survivors of stressful events. Post-traumatic stress disorder – PTSD – was defined in 1980 in the manual of mental disorders, produced by the American Psychiatric Association, as the development of characteristic symptoms following a psychologically traumatic happening outside the range of normal human experience.[15] The induction of PTSD, according to the psychiatrists, was not confined to experiences in combat, but could relate back to any traumatic ordeal, for instance, involvement in an accident, a natural disaster or a violent crime.[16]

In the aftermath of the Vietnam War extensive investigations were carried out to test the long-term psychological consequences on the veterans of the campaign. The Vietnam Experience Study, organized by the Centres for Disease Control, explored the mental condition of 15,000 ex-soldiers in a project which was completed in 1988. The study revealed that 15 percent of the men had suffered from PTSD since they had left the Army and that, years after the fighting had ended, about 14 percent of them had problems with alcohol abuse or dependence. The symptoms of PTSD most frequently occurring were nightmares, insomnia, "flashbacks" to the scenes of battle, a tendency to be easily startled, depression, anxiety and an emotional numbness. The investigators found little sign that many of the veterans had a drug problem. The Study did not seem to address the question whether or not some of the symptoms of PTSD were wholly or even partially related to service in Vietnam.[17]

Other investigations into the psychological consequences of the war were conducted by the Vietnam Veterans Readjustment Study and the Vietnam Veteran Outreach Programme. In addition, the Veterans Administration had arranged special mental health clinics where Vietnam veterans could attend for counselling. When the National Vietnam Memorial in Washington was dedicated during the winter of 1982 research was carried out to assess the mental and emotional effects of the ceremony on the veterans of the campaign. Ninety-four ex-servicemen took part in the study, some of whom had actually attended the dedication service. All of them reported that the event had caused a worsening of their PTSD-related symptoms and other psychiatric disturbances.[18]

Australia and New Zealand had become members of the South-East Asia Treaty Organization in the 1950s and both countries had sent contingents of troops to support the United States in Vietnam. A survey carried out twenty years after the end of the war among a sample of 573 New Zealand veterans of the campaign disclosed that some 20 percent of them were affected by PTSD. The researchers observed that this was a higher rate than had been found among American veterans, but the New Zealand soldiers, they said, were likely to have seen more action than their American allies. They added:

> Caution must be exercised when making comparisons between New Zealand and United States troops, however, as there were at least two important differences between these forces. First, New Zealand troops consisted primarily of regular soldiers specifically recruited for service in Vietnam, unlike the United States and Australian forces, which had higher proportions of conscripted soldiers serving in Vietnam. Second, the nature of the tour of duty was different. For United States troops, each serviceman was deployed on an individual 12 or 13 month rotational basis, whereas New Zealand and Australia units were deployed on a 6 or 12 month rotational basis.[19]

Chapter 20

At the beginning of their book *The Battle For The Falklands* Max Hastings and Simon Jenkins make the comment, "The Falkland Islands' misfortune has always been to be wanted more than they are loved."[1]

The first landing on these remote islands in the South Atlantic, 300 miles from the South American mainland, was made in 1690 by the captain of a British ship which had been blown off-course by a violent gale. They were then uninhabited and the captain did not remain there for long. On his return to England the group was named after Viscount Falkland who was the Treasurer of the Royal Navy at the time. In 1764 a French navigator formally claimed the islands in the name of the King of France and founded a small settlement on one of them. A year later the British claimed that the island were theirs and started their own settlement on a separate island. The French soon tired of maintaining a presence in the Falklands and they sold them to Spain in 1767. For economic reasons the British abandoned their desolate outpost in 1774, but the settlers left behind them a plaque asserting that the islands were still a British possession. The Spanish retained the settlement they had taken over from the French for another thirty-six years before they relinquished it in 1810 and moved their settlers back to the mainland. This had happened during a period when the predominance of Spain in South America was rapidly vanishing and the former Spanish colonies were on the verge of proclaiming their independence.

In 1820 the newly-created republic of Argentina laid claim to the Falklands as a part of its post-colonial inheritance from Spain. Shortly afterwards, a party of emigrants from Britain landed in the islands, supported by two warships, and declared that they were recovering British territory. Although the Argentinians vehemently protested at this incursion, their pretensions to sovereignty in the Falkland Islands were no less spurious than those of the British.

The Argentinians continued to maintain their claim to the Falklands – or the Malvinas as they call them – and repeatedly demanded that Britain should hand them back. Such a development became increasingly unlikely with the passage of time. In spite of the fact that the islands had no great commercial value or strategic importance, they had been designated a Crown Colony. The inhabitants were almost entirely of British origin and they made it abundantly clear that they wanted their homeland to remain a British dependency.

The dispute persisted into the twentieth century. In 1965 the General Assembly of the United Nations passed a Resolution calling on Britain and the Argentine to start negotiations immediately with a view to finding a peaceful solution to the controversy. Both nations agreed, and what turned out to be protracted and inconclusive talks between them were opened without delay. A hawkish section of the Argentinian General Staff was anxious to abandon the discussions and to take the islands by force. They were fortified in their arguments when the Argentinian Navy purchased from France a consignment of new French warplanes and airborne Exocet missiles.

The Falklands were virtually unprotected. The population of 1,800 could muster a part-time defence force of 120 men and a small detachment of Royal Marines was based at Port Stanley, the capital. At dawn on 2 April, 1982, an Argentinian invasion force landed on the coast a few miles from Port Stanley. A Commando unit hurried to Government House and captured the Governor, who ordered the hopelessly outnumbered Royal Marines to surrender. The news of the British capitulation was received with ecstatic rejoicing in the Argentine. Published photographs of the captive Marines lying on the ground, face-downwards with their arms stretched out, and guarded by triumphant Argentinian soldiers, seemed to encapsulate Britain's humiliation.

The next day the House of Commons was unanimous in its condemnation of the Argentinian invasion and Margaret Thatcher, the Prime Minister, gave an assurance that Britain would soon recapture the Falklands. Amid general approval she announced, "A large task force will sail as soon as preparations are complete."[2] It was obviously going to be an immensely difficult operation. The British armed forces, though small, were well-trained, well-equipped and highly efficient, but they would be fighting 8,000 miles away with no intermediate bases, against a nation with a powerful navy and air force, which could supply and reinforce its troops in the field from a distance of around 300 miles.

The first of the British Task Force ships sailed out of Portsmouth harbour on 5 April, having been assembled with remarkable speed. The place chosen for the initial landing was San Carlos on the opposite side of East Falkland island from Port Stanley. After a six-week sea voyage the first wave of troops started to wade ashore at dawn on 21 May. There were no Argentinian soldiers in the area because it was considered by their commanders that the attack would come from a different direction. It is a well-known military axiom that an invasion force is at its most vulnerable when it is still in the process of establishing a beachhead. It is therefore surprising that the Argentinians never mounted a single counter-attack on San Carlos, nor did they even send in any fighting patrols to harass the British units while they were still moving into position.

In a short time the build-up was completed and the invasion forces were ready to push into the interior. They made a two-prong advance, one column striking south towards Goose Green and the other heading across the island in the direction of Port Stanley. The Battle of Goose Green, fought principally by a battalion of the Parachute Regiment, resulted in a minor British victory. The other column had succeeded in reaching the outskirts of Port Stanley when, in the evening on 14 June, all the Argentinian forces in the Falklands laid down their arms and surrendered.

The struggle to recover the Falklands islands had lasted for twenty-four days and 28,000 men had taken part in it on the British side. Their losses had been 255 killed and 777 wounded.[3] A number of Royal Navy and Merchant Service ships involved in the operation were sunk or damaged, particularly by guided missiles. The Argentinian casualties were far greater.

It was estimated that only 2 percent of the British soldiers wounded in the Falklands were psychiatric casualties. This low figure had been attributed to various factors. The campaign was brief, the losses were

172

light, the fighting was offensive rather than defensive, the war was commended in Britain and the land-battles had ended in a series of victories.[4] On the other hand, it has been suggested that the official figures might have been somewhat illusory and that insufficient attention was given in the Task Force to the problem of war neurosis. Whether or not this criticism is valid, it is true that there were no mental health professionals serving with the Falklands army and that after the conflict was over it seems to have been too readily assumed that none of the returned troops would develop the symptoms of post-traumatic stress disorder in the future.[5] An ex-officer, who had been a captain in a Commando unit during the Falklands operations, alleged later that the Ministry of Defence had not done very much for the psychological casualties after they left the Army. The burden of caring for them, he said, had been left to the Services' charities.[6]

Five years after the end of the Falklands War a psychiatric study was carried out on a group of sixty-four veterans of the campaign, all of whom were still serving in the British Army. It was found that exactly 50 per cent of the men had symptoms of post-traumatic stress disorder, 22 per cent of them having the complete PTSD syndrome.[7] Another survey was undertaken around the same time by the District Psychologist for Lincoln on fifty-three Falklands veterans. He discovered that two-thirds of his subjects had stress symptoms associated with their experiences in the war. They told the psychologist that they had become less capable of dealing with the ordinary pressures of everyday life and they were troubled by insomnia, depression, nervousness and a gradual deterioration in their general health. Most of them complained about the lack of understanding and care they were receiving from the medical and social services.[8]

An orthopaedic surgeon who had tended the wounded as a Medical Officer in the Falklands has told how seven years after the end of the war he started to have panic attacks. He would suddenly break into a "complete and utter panic" for no apparent reason. It was a most horrific experience, he said. What frightened him most was the thought that he was losing his sanity.[9] Another veteran described how he began to have terrible nightmares about the fighting:

> They were happening two or three times a night, seven nights
> a week. I was at the receiving end of violence – incoming shells.

173

I could actually feel bullets hit by body. I could feel being hit by machine-gun fire, and this is what made me waken up and scream.

He sometimes dreamed of severely mutilated soldiers, with their hands, arms, legs and heads hanging off; people ripped to pieces, but still alive. "There are memories of carnage that will never leave me," he said. "They are as fresh in my mind today as they were in 1982, and I'll have them to my dying day."[10]

During 1991 the United States and Britain were involved together in the Gulf War in the Middle East. On 2 August, 1990, Iraq invaded the neighbouring state of Kuwait in order to acquire control of its lucrative oil fields. It was feared that Saddam Hussein, the Iraqi dictator, was also planning aggression on another of his neighbours, Saudi Arabia. At the end of August Hussein declared that Kuwait had become a province of Iraq, despite a United Nations Resolution demanding that he should withdraw his troops immediately.

As Hussein obviously intended to ignore the United Nations edict, the United States sent elements of its Rapid Deployment Force to Saudi Arabia and began to move naval units into the Persian Gulf. Offers of military support were made by other countries belonging to NATO, including various other Arab states.

At that time Iraq had the fifth largest army in the world, numbering about a million men. Although the soldiers were mostly conscripts they were battle-hardened from the Iraq-Iran war which lasted from 1980 to 1988. Their armaments included a formidable quantity of modern tanks and a powerful array of artillery. In addition, Hussein was known to have supplies of ballistic missiles and chemical weapons, including nerve gases, which he had used against the Iranians. The Iraqi air force had nearly 700 combat planes.

Another UN Resolution towards the end of 1990 gave Hussein until 15 January, 1991, to end his occupation of Kuwait. Before this deadline expired the UN Coalition forces, under the command of US General Norman Schwarzkopf, deployed in Saudi Arabia, ready for action. Schwarzkopf had a composite army made up of 450,000 Americans, 14,000 British, 10,000 French, as well as troops from Saudi Arabia, Egypt and several other Arab states. Hussein made it quite clear that he spurned the UN Resolution and on 15 January the Coalition forces began a retaliatory attack on Iraq, which had been carefully prepared and given the code name "Operation Desert Storm".

The first five weeks of Desert Storm consisted of an air offensive, aimed at the destruction of the whole of the Iraqi air-defence system – its air force, surface-to-air missiles, anti-aircraft guns and radar installations. This was intended to be a prelude to a ground assault. In a very short time the Coalition air forces had achieved complete air superiority with the loss of very few planes. The military offensive began on 24 February. Hussein had proclaimed that the Iraqis were engaging in a "holy war" and he threatened that if the UN forces invaded Iraq a prodigious battle would ensue. His troops were entrenched behind a network of minefields and anti-tank ditches, their forward defence line being supported by a dozen Armoured Divisions held in waiting as mobile reserves. The eight Republican Guard Divisions, the elite formations of Hussein's army, were not committed in the initial stages of the fighting.

The prodigious battle never happened. The Iraqi army collapsed at the first onslaught and fled in disarray, abandoning masses of armoured vehicles, guns and other equipment. Hussein was obliged to request a cease fire on 28 February, after the ground offensive had lasted a bare hundred hours. The casualties sustained by the Coalition forces during the whole campaign had been extremely light, amounting to 234 men killed, 148 of them Americans, and 479 wounded. The Iraqis had suffered far more heavily. It was estimated that about 100,000 of their men had been killed in the fighting.

Owing to the brevity of the battle, the absence of resolute opposition and the minimal casualty figures, the incidence of war neurosis among the British troops who fought in the Gulf was very low. However, nine months after the cease-fire sixty-two soldiers who had been attached to the Army War Graves Service during the campaign underwent voluntary psychiatric investigation. Their duties had been to recover dead bodies, both those of the allies and those of the enemy, to identify them and to prepare them for burial. Although this was essentially a non-combative task, these men were all fit and young, their average age being 28. It was found that 50 per cent had symptoms of psychological disturbance suggestive of post-traumatic stress disorder. Eleven of them had sought help from the professional welfare services on returning from the Gulf and seven had been referred to psychiatrists.[11]

There is little doubt that in some circumstances an isolated incident can generate war neurosis. On one occasion during the Gulf campaign a detachment of British troops was accidentally machine-gunned by low-flying American aircraft, causing casualties. Later on, the survivors were tested to discover whether or not the incident had left them with any mental or emotional after-effects. It was discovered that as many as 54 percent of them were manifesting one or more symptoms of PTSD.[12]

The Coalition armies in the Gulf War took special precautions against Hussein's possible use of chemical weapons and nerve gases. On the day of the cease-fire Professor Rick Gabriel discussed the reactions of a soldier who had to go into battle wearing protective clothing. He said:

> Clothes and hoods that save a man from lethal gas can make him more vulnerable to psychological breakdown. Once you don a chemical suit you increase the isolation of the soldier; he cannot hear very well, the lenses get fogged, he cannot see, and he cannot feel his body. Moreover, all he can hear is the pounding of his own heart.

Professor Gabriel added that it was believed in the United States Army that, after four hours in a chemical suit, a soldier's fighting efficiency was reduced by 60 percent.[13]

Many men and women who had served in the Gulf War claimed, when they returned home, that they were suffering from a mysterious illness which became known as "Gulf War Syndrome". The usual symptoms they reported included chronic fatigue, loss of memory, dizziness and aching joints. Some of them maintained that, in addition, they had contracted such serious complaints as kidney failure and motor neurone disease.[14] Even more disturbing was the assertion by some Gulf War Veterans' Associations that there had been at least sixty known cases of babies with abnormalities being born to men who had served in the campaign.[15] However, a London consultant who was a leading authority on birth defects did not

176

consider that the number of defective births among Gulf War veterans was unusually high.[16] In the United States around 17,000 soldiers, all of whom were still in the Army, had registered with the Pentagon as suffering from Gulf War Syndrome.[17] In Britain 4,000 men alleged that they had been stricken with the disease.[18]

The veterans believed that the Syndrome was caused by the so-called "cocktail of injections" they had been given to protect them against chemical and biological weapons and the tablets they had taken as an antidote to nerve gases. Both the American and the British Governments were sceptical about the existence of Gulf War Syndrome, but the Pentagon set up an enquiry into the veterans' claims and the Ministry of Defence commissioned an independent report on the disorder by the Royal College of Physicians. A medical specialist who had examined a number of the men concerned was of the opinion that there was "no evidence of a specific Gulf War illness" and that the patients, in reality, were affected with a condition brought on by mental stress.[19]

At the conclusion of their investigations the Royal College of Physicians reported that the range of diseases about which the men complained made it very difficult to conceive of a single cause. The Pentagon Enquiry reached the same conclusion. Their medical teams, they said, had uncovered no previously unknown serious illness unique to the Gulf War and no common underlying cause for the broad range of disorders recorded. Stephen Joseph, the United States Assistant Secretary of Defence, announcing these findings, said that the troops returning from the Gulf had suffered from a "complex mosaic of diseases", some of which could be traced to being in an extremely stressful and dangerous environment. Nearly one fifth of the veterans examined had had psychological problems.[20]

Further research into Gulf War Syndrome, carried out by scientists at Duke University in North Carolina and the University of Texas, led to the suggestion that a combination of the chemicals used to protect the soldiers from desert insects and their nerve tablets could have led to neurological damage.[21] The Ministry of Defence undertook to examine this new theory.[22]

Postscript

At the present time counselling or psychological debriefing is the accepted remedial therapy both for civilians and members of the armed forces who have encountered a particularly traumatic or stressful ordeal.

However, some doubts have been expressed regarding the value of such a process for the prevention or the treatment of war neurosis. A study carried out on a group of British soldiers suffering from PTSD after the Gulf conflict showed that their rate of recovery was exactly the same whether or not they had received immediate psychological debriefing after they had broken down.[1] According to Professor Beverley Raphael of the Department of Psychiatry at the University of Queensland the latest research has suggested that psychiatric casualties who are returned to the front line as "cured" may develop more severe forms of neurosis after a further spell in action.[2]

In the summer of 1995 the Duke of Edinburgh was interviewed on television about his experiences as a naval officer during the Second World War. He was asked how he had reacted when his shipmates were killed or wounded by enemy action. He replied:

> It was part of the fortunes of war. We didn't have counsellers rushing around every time somebody let off a gun asking, "Are you all right? Are you sure you don't have a ghastly problem?" You just got on with it.[3]

The modern soldiers in the armies of the Western Nations must accustom themselves to counsellers, forward psychiatric centres and welfare workers as a part of the contemporary battle scene. But in spite

178

of all these innovations, the incidence of PTSD resulting from recent conflicts has been higher than ever before. Some people might say that this was because the soldiers of today are less selfless and less resolute than their forbears; others might contend it is due to the fact that they have become more percipient and more conscious of the imbecile futility of war. Either of these views could be correct.

Notes

Chapter 1

1. Sir James Edmonds, *Military Operations, France and Belgium, Vol 1*. London, MacMillan, 1932
2. David Ascoli, *The Mons Star*, London, Harrap, 1981
3. Edmonds, op. cit.
4. Summary of First World War Capital Court Martial Cases, WO 93/49, Trial of Lance-Sergeant Walton, 12 March, 1915
5. *Manual of Military Law*, 1914, London H.M.S.O. 1914

Chapter 2

1. War Neurosis in the Battle of Marathon, Anon. *Mental Hygiene*, 1919, Vol 3, 676
2. *Battle for the Mind*, William Sargant, London, Heinemann, 1957
3. Nostalgia: a "forgotten" psychological disorder, George Rosen, *Psychological Medicine*, 1975, Vol 5, No. 4, 340
4. ib.
5. ib.
6. ib.
7. ib.
8. ib.
9. ib.
10. *The Irritable Heart of Soldiers*, R. McN. Wilson, British Medical Journal, 1916, Vol 1, 119–20
11. *War Neurosis*, John T. MacCurdy, Cambridge University Press, 1918
12. Wilson, op. cit.
13. An Early Case of Battle Hysteria, M.A. Patton, *British Journal of Psychiatry*, 1981, 138, 182–3
14. *The Face of Battle*, John Keegan, London, Cape, 1976

15. ib.
16. ib.
17. ib.
18. ib.
19. *Memoirs of the Military Career of John Ship*, London, T. Fisher Unwin, 1890 (First published 1829)
20. *Report for His Majesty's Commissioners for Inquiring into the System of Military Punishments in the Army*, London, H.M.S.O., 1836
21. ib.
22. *The Noise of Drums and Trumpets, W.H. Russell reports from the Crimea*, by Elizabeth Grey, London, Longman, 1971
23. *Mrs Duberly's Campaigns*, E.E.P. Tisdall, London, Jarrolds, 1963
24. *Feigned and Fictitious Diseases*, Hector Gavin, London, John Churchill, 1843 (Second Edition)

Chapter 3

1. *One Hundred Years of American Psychiatry: Military Psychiatry: The Civil War*, Albert Deutsch, New York, Columbia University Press, 1944
2. ib.
3. The Evils of Youthful Enlistments, De Witt C. Peters, *American Medical Times*, 1863, Vol 6, 75
4. *The Psychology and Physiology of Stress*, edited by Peter Bourne, New York, Academic Press, 1969
5. *Medical and Surgical History of the War of the Rebellion, Vol 1, Part 3*, Washington Government Printing Office, 1888
6. Nostalgia: a "forgotten" psychological disorder, George Rosen, *Pyschological Medicine*, 1975, Vol 5, No 4, 340
7. *Medical and Surgical History*, op. cit.
8. De Witt C. Peters, op. cit.
9. Deutsch, op. cit.
10. Bourne, op. cit.
11. The Irritable Heart of Soldiers, by R. McN. Wilson, *British Medical Journal, 1916, Vol 1*, 119
12. Deutsch, op. cit.
13. ib.
14. *Medical and Surgical History*, op. cit.
15. ib.
16. Bourne, op. cit.
17. *Medical and Surgical History*, op. cit.

18. *War Neurosis in the Civil War*, Frederick Peterson, The Proceedings of the Charaka Club, (New York), 1919, Vol 5, 9
19. ib.
20. ib.
21. Deutsch, op. cit.

Chapter 4

1. Madness in Armies in the Field, Anon., *British Medical Journal*, 1904, Vol 2, 30
2. *The Care and Treatment of Mental Disseases and War Neurosis ("Shell-Shock") in the British Army*, Dr Thomas W. Salmon, published by the Mental Hygiene War Work Committee, New York (no date given)
3. The Irritable Heart of Soldiers, R. McN. Wilson, *British Medical Journal* 1916, Vol. 1, 119
4. ib.
5. ib.
6. ib.
7. ib.
8. *Injuries of Nerves and Their Consequences*, S. Weir Mitchell, Philadelphia, J.B. Lippincott, 1872
9. George M. Beard and Neurasthenia, Eric T. Carlson, In: *Essays in the History of Psychiatry*, William S. Hall. Psychiatric Institute of the South Carolina Department of Mental Health, 1980
10. ib.
11. The Origins of War Neurosis, P.S. Ellis, *Journal of the Naval Medical Service, 1984, Vol 70*, 168
12. The Traumatic Neuroses, Thomas R. Glynn, *The Lancet, 1910*, Vol 2, 1332
13. *Railway and Other Injuries of the Nervous System*, John Eric Erichsen, London, Walton and Maberley, 1866
14. *Creating Traumatic Emotional Disorders Before and During World War I* Edward M. Brown, Clinical Assistant Professor, Department of Psychiatry and Human Behaviour, Brown University, Providence, R.I (undated, privately circulated)
15. Recent investigations into the Pathology of so-called Concussion of the Spine, James J. Putnam, *Boston Medical and Surgical Journal 1883, Vol 109*, 217
16. *Putnam, ib.*
17. *Brown, op. cit.*
18. *Glynn, op. cit.*

Chapter 5

1. *Introduction to Psychotherapy*, J.A. Hadfield, London, Allen and Unwin, 1967
2. ib.
3. ib.
4. ib.
5. ib.
6. *Essays in the History of Psychiatry, Culture, and Complex*, John Gach, Carolina, William S. Hall, Psychiatric Institute of South Carolina Department of Mental Health, 1980
7. Hadfield, op. cit.
8. ib.
9. ib.
10. War Neurosis and Cultural Change in England, 1914–22, Ted Bogacz, *Journal of Contemporary History, Vol 24* (1989), 227

Chapter 6

1. Deaths in Battle During The Last Century, Editorial, *British Medical Journal, 1904, Vol 2*, 31
2. Madness in Armies in the Field, Anon. *British Medical Journal, 1904, Vol 2*, 30
3. *A Soldier's Diary, South Africa, 1899–1901*, Murray Crosby-Jackson, London, Max Goschen, 1913
4. *A Civilian War Hospital*, Anthony H. Bowley and others, London, John Murray, 1901
5. *The Care and Treatment of Mental Diseases and War Neuroses ("Shell Shock") in the British Army*, Dr Thomas W. Salmon, published by The Mental Hygiene War Work Committee, New York city, (undated)
6. *The Impressions of a War Correspondent*, George Lynch, London, George Newnes, 1953
7. Some War Sequelae, Charles A. Morris, *The Lancet*, 1901, Vol 2, 1559
8. A Case from the Russo-Japanese War, Anon. *The Lancet*, 1905, Vol 1, 609
9. *The Russo-Japanese War: Medical and Sanitary Reports From the Officers Attached to the Japanese and Russian Forces in the Field*, London, War Office, 1908
10. *Mental and Nervous Diseases in the Russo-Japanese War*, Captain R.L. Richards, Military Surgeon, 1910, Vol. 26, 177
11. *Madness in Armies in the Fieldr, op. cit.*
12. *R.L. Richards, op. cit.*

13. *Neurosis of Military Men after a Campaign, Anon.*, The Lancet, 1907, Vol 1, 1740
14. ib.
15. ib.
16. R.L. Richards, op. cit.
17. *English Social History*, G.M. Trevelyan, London, Longmans, Green and Co., 1942
18. Vitai Lampada, Henry Newbolt, First published in 1898 in *The Island Race*

Chapter 7

1. These figures are taken from *History of the First World War*, B.H. Liddell Hart, London Book Club Associates, 1973 and *The Mons Star*, David Ascoli, London, Harrap, 1981
2. *English History 1914–1945*, A.J.P. Taylor, Oxford, Clarendon Press, 1965
3. ib.
4. *The Face of Battle*, John Keegan, London, Jonathan Cape, 1976
5. ib.
6. ib.
7. *The Care and Treatment of Mental Diseases and War Neurosis ("Shell-Shock") in the British Army*, Dr Thomas W. Salmon, published by The Mental Hygiene War Work Committee of the National Committee for Mental Hygiene, New York, undated
8. *Combat Neurosis*, Arthur P. Noyes and Lawrence C. Kolb, Philadelphia, W. Saunders Company, 1958
9. A Contribution to the Study of "Shell-Shock" by Charles S. Myers., *The Lancet*, 1915, Vol 1, 316
10. *Shell-Shock in France 1914–18*, Charles S. Myers, Cambridge, Cambridge University Press, 1940
11. Minds the Dead Have Ravished, Chris Feudtner, *History of Science*, 1993, Vol 31, Part 4, 377
12. The Traumatic Neuroses, T.R. Glynn, *The Lancet*, 1910, Vol 2, 1332
13. ib.
14. Anon. *The Lancet*, 1914, Vol 2, 1388
15. ib.
16. *War Neuroses*, John MacCurdy, Cambridge, Cambridge University Press, 1918
17. ib.
18. ib.
19. ib.

20. *Lectures on War Neurosis*, T.A. Ross, London, Edward Arnold, 1941
21. MacCurdy, op. cit.
22. Some Experiences in the German Red Cross, Clarence A. Neymann, *Mental Hygiene*, 1917, Vol 1., 392
23. ib.
24. Notes, Anon. *British Medical Journal*, 1914, Vol 2, 995

Chapter 8

1. *Military Operations, France and Belgium 1915, Vol 1*, Brigadier-General J.E. Edmonds, London, MacMillan, 1927
2. *1915 The Death of Innocence*, Lyn MacDonald, London, Headline, 1996
3. Lyn MacDonald, op. cit.
4. Edmonds, op. cit.
5. *History of the First World War*, B.H. Liddell Hart, London, Book Club Associates, 1973
6. Lyn MacDonald, op. cit.
7. ib.
8. ib.
9. Minds The Dead Have Ravished, Chris Feudtner, *History of Science*, 1993, Vol 31, Part 4, 377
10. War Neurosis and Cultural Change in England 1914–22, Ted Bogacz, *Journal of Contemporary History*, 1989, Vol 24, 277
11. *The Anatomy of Courage*, Lord Moran, London, Constable, 1945
12. Shell-Shock in France 1914–18. Based on a War Diary kept by Charles S. Myers, Cambridge, Cambridge University Press, 1940
13. Cases of Nervous and Mental Shock Observed in the Bash Hospitals in France, W.A. Turner, *British Medical Journal*, 1915, Vol 1, 833
14. ib.
15. ib.
16. Myers, op. cit.
17. ib.
18. ib.
19. Nerves and War: The Mental Treatment Bill, Anon., *The Lancet*, 1915, Vol 1, 919
20. Myers, op. cit.
21. ib.
22. Feudtner, op. cit.
23. *The Lancet*, 1915, Vol 1, op. cit.
24. *Nerve Injuries and Shock*, Wilfred Harris, Oxford, Oxford University Press, 1915

25. *Psychiatry in Modern Warfare*, Edward A. Strecker and Kenneth A. Appel, New York, The Macmillan Company, 1945
26. Anon., Lord Knutsford's Special Hospitals for Officers, *The Lancet*, 1915, Vol 2, 1155
27. ib.
28. ib.
29. Summary of First World War Capital Court-Martial Cases, Court-Martial of Private T. Docherty, 1 March, 1915
30. ib. Court-Martial of Private T. Harris, 12 June, 1915
31. ib. Court-Martial of Private A.D. Thompson, 14 July, 1915
32. ib. Court Martial of Private J. Docherty, 3 February, 1916
33. Myers, op. cit.

Chapter 9

1. *Goodbye to All That*, Robert Graves, London, Jonathan Cape, 1929
2. *1915. The Death of Innocence*, Lyn MacDonald, London, Headline Book Publishing, 1993
3. ib.
4. Nervous Manifestations Due to the Wind of High Explosives, Editorial, *The Lancet*, 1915, Vol 2, 348
5. Nervous Injuries Due to Shell Explosions, Anon., *The Lancet*, 1915, Vol 2, 550
6. Wellcome Institute for the History of Medicine Library; R.A.M.C. 739/20
7. Medical Notes in Parliament, Military Nervous and Mental Cases, *British Medical Journal*, 1915, Vol. 2, 515
8. ib.
9. King's Regulations and Orders for the Army 1912, re-printed with Amendments up to 1st August, 1914, London, H.M.S.O., 1914
10. *History of the First World War*, B.H. Liddell Hart, London, Book Club Associates, 1973
11. Lyn MacDonald, op. cit.
12. ib.
13. ib.
14. *The World Crisis 1911–1918*, Winston S. Churchill, London, Odhams Press, 1923
15. ib.
16. *Life and Letters of Raymond Asquith*, edited by John Joliffe, London, Collins, 1980
17. *Shell-Shock in France*, Charles S. Myers, Cambridge, Cambridge University Press, 1940

186

18. ib.

19. ib.

20. Medical Immpressions of the Gallipoli Campaign from a Battalion Medical Officer's Standpoint, J.N. MacBean Ross, *Royal Naval Journal of the Medical Services*, 1916, Vol 2, 313

21. ib.

22. *Medical Services. Diseases of the War*, edited by Major-General Sir W.G. Macpherson and others, London, H.M.S.O., 1923

23. *Shell-Shock: Commotional and Emotional Aspects*, André Léri, London, London University Press, 1919

24. ib.

25. German Experiences, Neurasthenia Among Soldiers, Anon., *British Medical Journal*, 1916, Vol 1, 464

26. Notes from German and Austrian Medical Journal, Disciplinary Treatment of Shell-Shock, Anon. *British Medical Journal*, 1916, Vol 2, 882

27. Memorandum on the Electrical Treatment of War Neurotics (1920), Sigmund Freud, *International Journal of Psychoanalysis*, 1957, 37, 16

28. ib.

29. ib.

Chapter 10

1. *Military Operations, France and Belgium, 1916, Vol 1*, Sir James Edmonds, London, Macmillan, 1932

2. A Discussion on Shell-Shock, Anon., *The Lancet*, 1916, Vol 1, 306

3. ib.

4. The Effects of High Explosives on the Central Nervous System, Fred W. Mott, *The Lancet*, 1916, Vol 1, 331

5. ib.

6. ib.

7. ib.

8. ib.

9. Neurasthenia and Shell-Shock, Anon., *The Lancet*, 1916, Vol 1, 627

10. *Medicine and Duty*, Harold Dearden, London, Heinemann, 1928

11. ib.

12. *The Anatomy of Courage*, Lord Moran, London, Constable, 1945

13. Summary of First World War Capital Courts Martial Cases, W.O. 93/49, Trial of Private A. Harris, 4 March, 1916

14. ib. Trial of Private W. Thompson, 4 April, 1916

15. ib. Trial of Private W. Roberts, 20 May, 1916

16. ib. Trial of Private A. Robinson, 28 April, 1916
17. Shock and the Soldier by G. Elliott Smith, *The Lancet*, 1916, Vol 1, 813
18. ib.
19. A Contribution to the Etiology of Shell-Shock, Harold Wiltshire, *The Lancet*, 1916, Vol 1, 1207
20. Edmonds, op. cit.
21. ib.
22. ib.
23. ib.
24. *The Somme*, Lyn Macdonald, London, Michael Joseph, 1983
25. ib.

Chapter 11

1. *English History 1914–1945*, A.J.P. Taylor, Oxford, Clarendon Press, 1965
2. *Military Operations France and Belgium 1916, Vol 1*, Sir James Edmonds, London, Macmillan, 1932
3. Minds the Dead Have Ravished, Chris Feudtner, *History of Science*, 1993, Vol 31, part 4, 377
4. *The Somme*, Lyn Macdonald, London, Michael Joseph, 1983
5. The Wellcome Institute for the History of Medicine, "Useless Men", RAMC 446/18
6. ib.
7. ib., "Officers – Fitness for Duty"
8. *The Anatomy of Courage*, Lord Moran, London, Constable, 1945
9. Macdonald, op. cit.
10. The Wellcome Institute for the History of Medicine, Court of Enquiry into the failure of a party of the 11th Border Regiment to carry out an attack on 10 July 1916, RAMC 446/18
11. *The Care and Treatment of Mental Diseases and War Neurosis ("Shell-Shock") in the British Army*, Dr Thomas W. Salmon, The Mental Hygiene War Work Committee of the National Committee for Mental Hygiene, New York City, (undated)
12. *Shell-Shock in France 1914–18*, Charles S. Myers, Cambridge University Press, 1940
13. ib.
14. ib.
15. The Treatment of Cases of Shell-Shock in an Advanced Neurological Centre, William Brown, *The Lancet*, 1918, Vol 2, 197
16. ib.
17. Shock and the Soldier, G. Elliott Smith, *The Lancet*, 1916, Vol 1, 853

18. The Predisposing Factors of War Psycho-Neurosis, Julian M. Wolfsohn, *The Lancet*, 1918, Vol 1, 177
19. Summary of First World War Capital Court-Martial Cases, WO 93/49. Trial of Private H.J. Farr, 10 October, 1916
20. WO 93/49, op. cit. Trial of 2nd Lieutenant E.S. Poole, 21 November, 1916
21. Elliott Smith, op. cit.

Chapter 12

1. *Medical Services; Diseases of the War*, edited by Major-General Sir W.G. Macpherson and Others, H.M.S.O., 1923
2. ib.
3. *Minds the Dead Have Ravished*, Chris Feudtner, History of Science 1993, Vol 31, Part 4, 377
4. Macpherson, op. cit.
5. ib.
6. ib.
7. Some Notes on Battle Psychoneurosis, E. Fryer Ballard, *Journal of Mental Science*, July, 1917, 400
8. *History of the First World War*, B.L. Liddell Hart, London, Book Club Associates, 1973
9. *Memoirs of an Infantry Officer*, Siegfried Sassoon, London, Faber & Faber, 1936
10. *The World Crisis*, Winston S. Churchill, London, Odhams Press, 1923
11. *The Care and Treatment of Mental Diseases and War Neurosis ("Shell-Shock") in the British Army*, Dr Thomas W. Salmon. The Medical Hygiene War Work Committee, Committee for Mental Hygiene, New York City, (undated)
12. ib.
13. ib.
14. ib.
15. *One Hundred Years of American Psychiatry: Military Psychiatry, World War I, 1917–1918*, Edward A. Strecker, New York, Columbia University Press, 1944, and Treatment of War Neurosis in Advanced Sanitary Formations, Anon., *Mental Hygiene*, 1919, Vol 3, No. 1, 1
16. Strecker, op. cit.
17. Summary of First World War Court Martial Cases, WO 93/49. Trial of Private J. Bennett, 16 August, 1916
18. ib., Trial of Private J. Higgins, 19 August, 1916
19. ib., Trial of Lance-Corporal W.A. Moon, 11 November, 1916

20. ib., Trial of Private H. Flynn, 29 October, 1916
21. ib., Trial of Private H. Poole, 11 October, 1916
22. ib., Trial of Private R.G. Pattison, 10 June, 1917
23. ib., Trial of Private F.M. Barratt, 21 June, 1917

Chapter 13
1. *The Face of Battle*, John Keegan, London, Jonathan Cape, 1976
2. *Military Operations, France and Belgium, 1917*, Brigadier-General J.E. Edmonds, London, MacMillan, 1927
3. *Shell-Shock in France, 1914–18*, Charles S. Myers, Cambridge, Cambridge University Press, 1940
4. ib.
5. *The Lancet*, 1917, Vol 2., Anon., Treatnent of Neurasthenic Soldiers, 143
6. *The Lancet*, 1917, Vol 2, Anon., House of Commons Questions, 262
7. *History of the First World War*, B.H. Liddell Hart, London, Book Club Associates, 1973
8. ib.
9. *Shell-Shock in France 1914–18*, Charles S. Myers, Cambridge, Cambridge University Press, 1940
10. ib.
11. ib.
12. ib.
13. *The Care and Treatment of Mental Diseases and War Neuroses ("Shell-Shock" in the British Army*, Dr Thomas W. Salmon. Published by The Medical Hygiene War Work Committee of the National Committee for Mental Hygiene, New York City, (undated)
14. Myers, op. cit.
15. Liddell Hart, op. cit.
16. Edmonds, op. cit.
17. Liddell Hart, op. cit.
18. *Medical Services; Diseases of the War*, edited by Major-General Sir W.G. Macpherson and others, London, H.M.S.O., 1923
19. House of Commons, Oral Answers, 31 October, 1917
20. ib.
21. Summary of First World War Capital Court Martial cases WO 93/49, Trial of Private Stanley Stewart, 12 August, 1917
22. House of Commons, Oral answers, 14 December, 1917
23. ib.
24. WO 93/49, op. cit., Trial of Private Charles McColl, 27 November, 1917
25. ib., Trial of Private Hector Dalande, 4 February, 1918

26. ib., Trial of Private Charles Kirman, 7 September, 1917
27. ib., Trial of Private Frederick Gore, 8 September, 1917

Chapter 14

1. *Sherston's Progress*, Siegfried Sassoon, London, The Folio Society, 1974
2. *Medical Services; Diseases of the War*, edited by Major-General W.G. Macpherson and others, London, H.M.S.O., 1923
3. *Medicine and Duty*, Harold Dearden, London, Heinemann, 1928
4. Report of the War Office Committee of Enquiry into "Shell-Shock", London, H.M.S.O., 1922
5. Autobiographical fragments by Dr H.W. Hills written in 1970 and unpublished
6. *One Hundred Years of American Psychiatry. Military Psychiatry: World War I 1917–1918*, Edward A. Strecker, New York, Columbia University Press, 1944, and *Psychiatry in Modern Warfare*, Edward A. Strecker and Kenneth E. Appel, New York, The Macmillan Company, 1945
7. *Mental Hygiene*, Editorial, 1919, Vol 3, No. 1
8. Strecker, op. cit.
9. *The Psychology and Physiology of Stress*, edited by Peter G. Bourne, New York, Academic Press, 1969
10. Strecker and Appel, op. cit.
11. Strecker, op. cit.
12. The Treatment of War Neuroses, Editorial, *British Medical Journal*, 1917, Vol. 1, 775
13. Preface by W.H.R. Rivers to *War Neurosis* by John T. MacCurdy, Cambridge, Cambridge University Press, 1918
14. Freud's Psychology and the Unconscious, W.H.R. Rivers, *The Lancet*, 1917, Vol 1, 912
15. W.H.R. Rivers and the Anthropology of Psychiatry, Anon., *Social Science and Medicine*, 1993, Vol 36, iii
16. Minds The Dead Have Ravished, Chris Feudtner, *History of Science*, Vol 31, Part 4, 377
17. *Medical Services, Diseases of the War*, op. cit.
18. ib.
19. ib.
20. *Memoirs of an Infantry Officer*, Siegfried Sassoon, London, Faber & Faber, 1930 and Biography of Siegfried Sassoon, Dictionary of National Biography 1961–1970, Oxford University Press, 1974
21. Sassoon, op. cit.
22. *Sherston's Progress*, Siegfried Sassoon, London, Folio Society, 1974

23. ib.
24. ib.
25. ib.
26. Wilfred Owen: His Recovery from "Shell-Shock" by Jennifer Breen, *Notes and Queries*, July 1976, 301

Chapter 15

1. House of Commons, oral answers, 19 February, 1918
2. ib.
3. House of Commons, Army Estimates Debate, 19 February, 1918
4. House of Commons, Consolidated Fund Bill, Third Reading, 14 March, 1918
5. *Medical Services: Diseases of the War*, edited by Major-General Sir W.G. Macpherson and others, London, H.M.S.O., 1923
6. ib.
7. *Military Operations, France and Belgium, 1918*, Brigadier-General J.E. Edmonds, London, MacMillan, 1927
8. ib.
9. Summary of First World War Capital Court Martial Cases, WO 93/49, Trial of Private J. Seymour, 12 January, 1918
10. ib. Trial of Private F.C. Butcher, 23 July, 1918
11. ib. Trial of Private J. Bateman, 30 August, 1918
12. ib. Trial of Private P. Murphy, 19 August, 1918
13. ib. Trial of Private E. Jackson, 16 October, 1918
14. Macpherson, op. cit.
15. ib.
16. ib.
17. ib.
18. *The Face of Battle*, John Keegan, London, Jonathan Cape, 1976
19. MacPherson, op. cit.
20. ib.
21. ib.
22. War Neurosis and Cultural Change in England, Ted Bogacz, *Journal of Contemporary History*, Vol 24 (1989), 227
23. Letter from Millais Culpin, *The Lancet*, 1944, Vol 2, 546
24. *One Hundred Years of American Psychiatry, Military Psychiatry: World War I*, Edward A. Strecker, New York, Columbia University Press, 1944
25. Some Problems of Disabled Ex-Service Men Three Years After the Armistice, Thomas W. Salmon, *Mental Hygiene*, 1921, Vol 6, No. 1
26. ib.

27. *One Hundred Years of American Psychiatry*, op. cit. World War II, Albert Deutsch
28. Salmon, op. cit.
29. Minds the Dead Have Ravished, Chris Feudtner, *History of Science*, 1993, Vol 31, part 4, 377
30. Information supplied by Combat Stress, Ex-Services Mental Welfare Society

Chapter 16

1. House of Lords, 28 April, 1920
2. Report of the War Office Committee of Enquiry into "Shell-Shock", CMD 1734, London, H.M.S.O., 1922
3. ib.
4. ib.
5. ib.
6. ib.
7. ib.
8. ib.
9. ib.
10. ib.
11. ib.
12. ib.
13. ib.
14. ib.
15. ib.
16. ib.
17. ib.
18. ib.
19. ib.
20. ib.
21. ib.
22. ib.
23. ib.
24. ib.
25. ib.

Chapter 17

1. *Statistics of the Military Effort of the British Empire During the Great War*, London, H.M.S.O., 1922
2. *Report of the Interdepartmental Committee on Proposed Disciplinary Amendments of the Army and Air Force Act*, London, H.M.S.O., 1925

3. House of Commons, Army and Air Force (Annual) Bill, Committee Stage, 1 April, 1925
4. House of Commons, Army and Air Force (Annual) Bill, Committee Stage, 3 April, 1930
5. *The Face of Battle*, by John Keegan, London, Jonathan Cape, 1976
6. Major-General Frank Richardson in a postscript to *For The Sake of Example*, Anthony Babington, London, Leo Cooper, 1983
7. ib.
8. *The Second World War, Vol 1*, Winston S. Churchill, London, Cassell, 1948
9. ib. Vol. 2
10. ib.
11. Keegan, op. cit.
12. Acute War Neuroses by William Sargant and Eliot Slater, *Lancet*, 1940, Vol 2, 1
13. Psychiatric Casualties From the Normandy Beach-Head, Charles Anderson, Manfred Jeffrey and M.N. Pai, *The Lancet*, 12 August, 1944
14. Sargent and Eliot, op. cit.
15. ib.
16. ib.
17. ib.
18. Neurosis, As Viewed by a Regimental Medical Officer, A.D. Leigh, Lieutenant, RAMC, *The Lancet*, 22 March, 1941
19. *English History 1914–1945*, A.J.P. Taylor, Oxford, Clarendon Press, 1965
20. Winston S. Churchill, op. cit., Vol 3
21. ib.

Chapter 18

1. *English History 1914–1945*, A.J.P. Taylor, Oxford, Clarendon Press, 1965
2. *The Second World War*, Winston S. Churchill, Vol. 3, London, Cassell, 1948
3. *The Psychology and Physiology of Stress*, edited by Peter G. Bourne, New York, Academic Press, 1969
4. *One Hundred Years of American Psychiatry; Military Psychiatry, World War II 1941–1943*, Albert Deutsch, New York, Published for the American Psychiatric Association, Columbia University Press, 1944
5. ib.
6. *Psychiatry in Modern Warfare*, Edward A. Strecker and Kenneth E. Appel, New York, The Macmillan Company, 1945
7. Taylor, op. cit.

8. Churchill, op. cit., Vol 4

9. ib.

10 The observations are based on the author's own experience as an infantry officer in the Second World War.

11. *The Face of Battle*, John Keegan, London, Jonathan Cape, 1976

12. *Modern Clinical Psychiatry*, Arthur P. Noyes and Lawrence C. Kolb, Philadelphia, W. Saunders Company, 1958

13. ib.

14. Deutsch, op. cit.

15. ib.

16. Bourne, op. cit.

17. ib.

18. Strecker and Appel, op. cit.

19. Noyes and Kolb, op. cit.

20. Keegan, op. cit.

21. Strecker and Appel, op. cit.

22. Bourne, op. cit.

23. *War Neuroses in North Africa. The Tunisian Campaign, January–May 1943*, Lieut-Colonel Roy R. Grinker and Captain John P. Spiegel, New York, Josiah Macy Jr. Foundation, 1943

24. ib.

25. ib.

26. Churchil, op. cit., Vol 5

27. Morale in Battle – The Medical and The Military, Field Marshal Lord Carver, *Journal of the Royal Society of Medicine*, 1989, Vol. 82, 67

28. ib.

29. Deutsch, op. cit.

30. Churchill, op. cit., Vol 6

31. Observation based on the author's personal experience

32. Psychiatric Casualties From the Normandy Beachhead, Charles Anderson, Mandred Jeffrey and M.N. Pai, *The Lancet*, 1944, Vol 2, 218

33. Keegan, op. cit.

34. The Northfield Experiments, Tom Harrison and David Clarke, *British Journal of Psychiatry*, 1992, 160, 698

35. ib.

36. Bourne, op. cit.

37. ib.

38. *Psychological Disorders in Flying Personnel of the Royal Air Force, Investigated During the War 1939–1945*, London, H.M.S.O., 1947

39. ib.

40. ib.

41. Fear Factors in Flying Personnel, W.A.S. Falla, *The Journal of Mental Science*, 1947, Vol 93, 43
42. Psychological Disturbance Some Suffer After Being involved in War, Channel Four Television, Despatches, 27 February 1991
43. Deutsch, op. cit.
44. *War Neuroses in North Africa. The Tunisian Campaign*, Rory Grinker and John P. Spiegel, Josiah Macy Jr. Foundation, 1943
45. ib.

Chapter 19

1. Combat Stress News, Spring 1996 Issue, No. 16
2. Far East Veterans Imprisoned by Grief 50 Years On, Emma Wilkins, *The Times*, 15 August, 1995
3. From Shell Shock to Combat Fatigue, Dr Simon Wessely, *The Times*, 4 May, 1995
4. ib.
5. *The Psychology and Physiology of Stress*, edited by Peter G. Bourne, New York, Academic Press, 1969
6. ib.
7. ib.
8. Last of the Brahmins, William Rees-Mogg, *The Times*, 19 September, 1996
9. *The Times*, Leading Article, 1 May, 1995
10. Bourne, op. cit.
11. Professor Rick Gabriel, Psychological Disturbances Some Suffer After Being Involved in War, Despatches, Channel Four Television, 27 February, 1991
12. Bourne, op. cit.
13. ib.
14. Vietnam's Psychological Toll by Leslie Roberts, *Science*, 1988, 241, 159
15. Symptoms of Post-traumatic Stress Disorder in Falklands Veterans Five Years After the Conflict, L.S. O'Brien and S.J. Hughes, *British Journal of Psychiatry*, 1991, 159, 135
16. ib.
17. Roberts, op. cit.
18. A Survey of the Effect of the Vietnam Dedication on Psychiatric Symptoms in Vietnam Veterans, John P. Parson and others, *Military Medicine*, 1988, 135, 11, 578
19. Relation of Military Service Variables to Post-traumatic Stress Disorder in New Zealand Vietnam War Veterans, Carol Vincent, Kerry Chamberlain and Nigel Long, *Military Medicine*, 1994, Vol 159, 322

Chapter 20

1. *The Battle For The Falklands*, Max Hastings and Simon Jenkins, London, Michael Joseph, 1983
2. ib.
3. ib.
4. Symptoms of Post-traumatic Stress Disorder in Falklands Veterans Five Years After the Conflict, L.S. O'Brien and S.J. Hughes, *British Journal of Psychiatry*, 1991, 159, 135
5. ib.
6. Hugh McManners, Psychological Disturbances Some Suffer After Being Involved in War, Despatches, Channel Four Television, 27 February, 1991
7. O'Brien and Hughes, op. cit.
8. Roderick Order, Despatches, op. cit.
9. Steven Hughes, ib.
10. Tom Howard, ib.
11. Psychological Sequelae Following the Gulf War, Martin P. Deahl, Adrian B. Gillham, Jarice Thomas, Margaret M. Searle, and Michael Srinivasan, *British Journal of Psychiatry* (1994), 165, 160
12. ib.
13. Professor Nick Gabriel, Despatches, op. cit.
14. *The Times*, 31 January, 1996
15. ib.
16. ib.
17. ib.
18. *The Times*, 4 April, 1996
19. *The Times*, 17 January, 1995
20. *The Times*, 4 April, 1996
21. *The Times*, 16 April, 1996
22. *The Times*, 7 October, 1996

Postscript

1. Psychological Sequelae Following the Gulf War, Martin P. Deahl, Adrian B. Gillham, Janice Thomas, Margaret M. Searle, and Michael Srinivasan, *British Journal of Psychiatry* (1994), 165, 160
2. Does Debriefing After Psychological Trauma Work? by Professor Beverly Raphael and Professor Lenore Meldrum, *British Medical Journal*, 1995 Vol 310, 1479
3. *The Times*, 15 August, 1995

Bibliography

BOOKS

Ascoli, David, *The Mons Star*, London, Harrap, 1981

Bourne, Peter (Editor), *The Psychology and Physiology of Stress*, New York, Academic Press, 1969

Bowley, Anthony H. and others, *A Civilian War Hospital*, London, John Murray, 1901

Carlson, Eric T., *George Beard and Neurasthenia* (in *Essays on the History of Psychiatry*) Carolina, William S. Hall, Psychiatric Institute of the South Carolina Department of Mental Health, 1980

Churchill, Winston S., *The Second World War*, London, Cassell, 1948

Churchill, Winston S., *The World Crisis 1911–1918*, London, Odhams Press, 1923

Dearden, Harold, *Medicine and Duty*, London, Heinemann, 1928

Deutsch, Albert, *One Hundred Years of American Psychiatry: The Civil War*, New York, Columbia University Press, 1944

Edmonds, Brigadier-General J.E., *Military Operations, France and Belgium*, London, Macmillan, 1927

Erichsen, John Eric, *Railway and Other Injuries of the Nervous System*, London, Walton and Marberley, 1866

Gach, John, *Essays in the History of Psychiatry, Culture, and Complex*, Carolina, William S. Hall, Psychiatric Institute of the South Carolina Department of Mental Health, 1980

Gavin, Hector, *Feigned and Fictitious Diseases*, London, John Churchill, 1843 (Second Edition)

Graves, Robert, *Goodbye to All That*, London, Jonathan Cape, 1929

Grey, Elizabeth, *The Noise of Drums and Trumpets: W.H. Russell Reports from the Crimea*, London, Longman, 1971

Grinker, Lt-Col Roy R. and Spiegel, Capt John P., *War Neuroses in North Africa, The Tunisian Campaign January–May 1943*, New York, Josiah Macy Jr Foundation, 1943

Hadfield, J.A., *Introduction to Psychotherapy*, London, Allen and Unwin, 1967

Harris, Wilfred, *Nerve Injuries and Shock*, Oxford University Press, 1915

Hastings, Max, and Jenkins, Simon, *The Battle for the Falklands*, London, Michael Joseph, 1983

Joliffe, John, *Life and Letters of Raymond Asquith*, London, Collins, 1980

Keegan, John, *The Face of Battle*, London, Cape, 1976

Léri, André, *Shell-Shock, Commotional and Emotional Aspects*, London, London University Press, 1919

Liddell Hart, B.H., *History of the First World War*, London, Book Club Associates, 1973

Lynch, George, *The Impressions of a War Correspondent*, London, George Newnes, 1953

MacCurdy, John C., *War Neurosis*, Cambridge University Press, 1918

MacDonald, Lyn, *The Death of Innocence*, London, Headline, 1993

MacDonald, Lyn, *The Somme*, London, Michael Joseph, 1983

Macpherson, Maj Gen Sir W.G. and others (Editors), *Medical Services, Diseases of The War*, HMSO, 1923

Mitchell, S. Weir, *Injuries of Nerves and Their Consequences*, Philadelphia, J.P. Lippincott, 1872

Moran, Lord, *The Anatomy of Courage*, London, Constable, 1945

Myers, Charles S., *Shell-Shock in France 1914–18*, Based on a War Diary kept by Charles S. Myers, Cambridge University Press, 1940

Noyes, Arthur P. and Kolb, Lawrence, *Combat Neurosis*, Philadelphia, W. Saunders Company, 1958

Noyes, Arthur P. and Kolb, Lawrence, *Modern Clinical Psychiatry*, Philadelphia, W. Saunders Company, 1958

Richardson, Maj-Gen Frank, Postscript to *For the Sake of Example* by Anthony Babington, London, Leo Cooper, 1983

Rivers, W.H.R., Preface to *War Neurosis* by John MacCurdy, Cambridge, Cambridge University Press, 1918

Ross, T.A., *Lectures of War Neurosis*, Edward Arnold, 1941

Salmon, Dr Thomas W., *The Care and Treatment of Mental Diseases and War Neurosis ('Shell-Shock') in the British Army*, New York, The Mental Hygiene War Work Committee (no date given)

Sargant, William, *Battle for the Mind*, London, Heinemann, 1957

Sassoon, Siegfried, *Memoirs of An Infantry Officer*, London, Faber & Faber, 1930

Sassoon, Siegfried, *Sherston's Progress*, London, The Folio Society, 1974

Ship, John, *Memoirs of the Military Career of John Ship*, London, T. Fisher Unwin, 1890 (first published 1829)

Strecker, Edward A. and Appel, Kenneth A., *Psychiatry in Modern Warfare*, New York, The Macmillan Company, 1945

Strecker, Edward A., *One Hundred Years of American Psychiatry: Military Psychiatry: World War I 1917–1918*, New York, Columbia University Press, 1944

Taylor, A.J.P., *English History 1914–1945*, Oxford, Clarendon Press, 1965

Tisdall, E.E.P., *Mrs Duberly's Campaigns*, London, Jarrolds, 1963

Trevelyan, G.M., *English Social History*, London, Longmans, Green & Co, 1942

ARTICLES

Anon, 'War Neurosis in the Battle of Marathon', *Mental Hygiene*, 1919, Vol 3, 676

Anon, 'Madness in Armies in the Field', *British Medical Journal*, 1904, Vol 2, 30

Anon, 'A Case from the Russo-Japanese War', *Lancet*, 1905, Vol 1, 609

Anon, 'Neurosis of Military Men after a Campaign', *Lancet*, 1907, Vol 1, 1740

Anon, Notes, *British Medical Journal*, 1914, Vol 2, 995

Anon, 'Nerves and War, The Mental Treatment Bill', *Lancet*, 1915, Vol 1, 919

Anon, 'Lord Knutsford's Special Hospitals for Officers', *Lancet*, 1915, Vol 2, 1155

Anon, 'Medical Notes in Parliament, Military Nervous and Mental Cases', *British Medical Journal*, Vol 2, 515

Anon, 'German Experiences, Neurasthenia Among Soldiers', *British Medical Journal*, 1916, Vol 1, 464

Anon, 'Notes from German and Austrian Medical Journals, Disciplinary Treatment of Shell-Shock', *British Medical Journal*, 1916, Vol 2, 882

Anon, 'A Discussion on Shell-Shock', *Lancet*, 1916, Vol 1, 306

Anon, 'Neurasthenia and Shell-Shock', *Lancet*, 1916, Vol 1, 627

Anon, 'Treatment of Neurasthenic Soldiers', *Lancet*, 1917, Vol 2, 143

Anon, 'House of Commons Questions', *Lancet*, 1917, Vol 1, 262

Anon, 'W.H.R. Rivers and the Anthropology of Psychiatry', *Social Science and Medicine*, 1993, Vol 36, 3

Anderson, Charles, Manfred, Jeffrey and Pai, M.N., 'Psychiatric Casualties from the Normandy Beach-Head', *Lancet*, 1944, Vol 2, 218

Ballard, E. Fryer, 'Some Notes on Battle Psychoneurosis', *Journal of Medical Science*, July, 1917, 400

Bogacz, Ted, 'War Neurosis and Cultural Change in England 1914–22', *Journal of Contemporary History*, 1989, Vol 24, 227

Breen, Jennifer, 'Wilfred Owen: His Recovery from "Shell-Shock"', *Notes and Queries*, July, 1976, 301

Brown, Edward M., Clinical Assistant Professor, Department of Psychiatry and Human Behaviour, Brown University, Providence, RI, 'Creating Emotional Disorders Before and During World War I', privately circulated and undated

Brown, William, 'The Treatment of Cases of Shell-Shock in an Advanced Neurological Centre', *Lancet*, 1918, Vol 2, 197

Carver, Field Marshal Lord, 'Morale in Battle, The Medical and The Military', *Journal of the Royal Society of Medicine*, 1989, Vol 82, 67

Culpin, Millais, letter, *Lancet*, 1944, Vol 2, 546

Deahl, Martin P., Gillham, Adrian G., Thomas, Janice, Searle, Margaret M. and Srinivasan, Michael, 'Psychological Sequelae, Following the Gulf War', *British Journal of Psychiatry*, 1994, 165, 60

Editorial, 'Deaths in Battle During the Last Century', *British Medical Journal*, 1904, Vol 2, 31

Editorial, 'Nervous Manifestations Due to the Wind of High Explosives', *Lancet*, 1915, Vol 2, 348

Editorial, *Mental Hygiene*, 1919, Vol 3, No 1

Editorial, The Treatment of War Neuroses, *British Medical Journal*, 1917, Vol 1, 775

Ellis, P.S., 'The Origins of War Neurosis', *Journal of the Medical Naval Service*, 1984, Vol 70, 168, 1

Feudtner, Chris, 'Minds the Dead Have Ravished', *History of Science*, 1993, Vol 31, Part 4, 377

Freud, Sigmund, 'Memorandum on the Electrical Treatment of War Neurotics' (1920) *International Journal of Psychoanalysis*, 1957, 37, 16

Glyn, Thomas R., 'The Traumatic Neuroses', *Lancet*, 1910, Vol 2, 1332

Harrison, Tom, and Clarke, David, 'The Northfield Experiments', *British Journal of Psychiatry*, 1992, 160, 698

Leigh, A.D., Lieutenant, RAMC, 'Neurosis – As Viewed by a Regimental Medical Officer', *Lancet*, 22 March 1941

Morris, Charles A., 'Some War Sequelae', *Lancet*, 1905, Vol 1, 609

Mott, Fred W., 'The Effects of High Explosives on the Central Nervous System', *Lancet*, 1916, Vol 1, 331

Myers, Charles S., 'A Contribution to the Study of Shell-Shock', *Lancet*, 1915, Vol 1, 316

Neyman, Clarence A., 'Some Experiences in the German Red Cross', *Mental Hygiene*, 1917, Vol 1, 392

O'Brien, L.S. and Hughes, S.J., 'Symptoms of Post-traumatic Stress Disorder in Falklands Veterans Five Years after the Conflict', *British Journal of Psychiatry*, 1991, 159, 135

Parsons, John P., and others, 'A Survey of the Effects of the Vietnam Dedication on Psychiatric Symptoms in Vietnam Veterans', *Military Medicine*, 1988, 153, 11, 578

Patton, M.A., 'An Early Case of Battle Hysteria', *British Journal of Psychiatry*, 1981, 138, 182

Peters, de Witt, C., 'The Evils of Youthful Enlistments', *American Medical Times*, 1863, Vol 6, 75

Peterson, Frederick, 'War Neurosis in the Civil War', The Proceedings of the Charaka Club (New York), 1919, vol 5, 9

Putnam, James J., 'Recent Investigations into the Pathology of the so-called Concussion of the Spine', *Boston Medical and Surgical Journal*, 1883, Vol 109, 217

Raphael, Professor Beverley and Lenore, Professor Meldrum, 'Does Debriefing After Psychological Trauma Work?' *British Medical Journal*, 1995, Vol 310, 1479

Rees-Mogg, Lord, 'Last of the Brahmins', *The Times*, 19 September, 1996

Richards, Captain R.L., 'Mental and Nervous Disorders in the Russo-Japanese War', *Military Surgeon*, 1910, Vol 26, 177

Rivers, W.H.R., 'Freud's Psychology of the Unconscious', *Lancet*, 1917, Vol. 1, 912

Roberts, Leslie, 'Vietnam's Psychological Toll', *Science*, 1988, 241, 159

Rosen, George, 'Nostalgia: a 'forgotten' Psychological Disorder', *Psychological Medicine*, 1975, Vol 5, no 4, 340

Ross, J.M. MacBean, 'Medical Impressions of the Gallipoli Campaign from a Battalion Officer's Standpoint', *Royal Naval Journal of the Medical Services*, 1916, Vol 2, 313

Salmon, Thomas W., 'Some Problems of Disabled Ex-Service Men Three Years After the Armistice', *Mental Hygiene*, 1921, Vol 2, 1

Sargant, William and Slater, Eliot, 'Acute War Neuroses', *Lancet*, 1940, Vol 2, 1

Smith, T. Eliot, 'Shock and the Soldier', *Lancet*, 1916, Vol 1, 813

Turner, W.A., 'Cases of Nervous and Mental Shock Observed in Base Hospitals in France', *British Medical Journal*, 1915, Vol 1, 833

Vincent, Carol, Chamberlain, Kerry and Long, Nigel, 'Relation of Military Service Variables to Post-traumatic Stress Disorder in New Zealand Vietnam War Veterans', *Military Medicine*, 1994, Vol 159, 322

Wilkins, Emma, 'Far East Veterans Imprisoned by Grief Fifty Years On', *The Times*, 15 August, 1995

Wiltshire, Harold, 'A Contribution to the Etiology of Shell-Shock', *Lancet*, 1916, Vol 1, 1207

Wilson, R.McN., 'The Irritable Heart of Soldiers', *British Medical Journal*, 1916, Vol 1, 119

Wolfsohn, Julian M., 'The Predisposing Factors of War Psycho-Neurosis', *Lancet*, 1918, Vol 1, 177

OFFICIAL REPORTS AND MISCELLANEOUS

Report from His Majesty's Commissioners For Inquiring into the System of Military Punishments in the Army, London, HMSO, 1836

The Russo-Japanese War: Medical and Sanitary Reports from the Officers Attached to the Japanese and Russian Forces in the Field, London, War Office, 1908

Report of the War Office Committee of Enquiry into Shell-Shock, London, HMSO, 1922

Statistics of the Military Effort of the British Empire during the Great War, London, HMSO, 1922

Medical Services: Diseases and the Great War, Edited by Major-General Sir W.G. Macpherson and others, London, HMSO, 1923

Report of the Interdepartmental Committee on Proposed Disciplinary Amendments to the Army and Air Force Acts, London, HMSO, 1925

Psychological Disorders in Flying Personnel of the Royal Air Force – Investigated during the War 1939–1945, London, HMSO, 1947

Medical and Surgical History of the War of the Rebellion, Washington Government Printing Office, 1888

Manual of Military Law 1914, London, HMSO, 1914

King's Regulations and Orders for the Army 1912, reprinted with amendments up to 1 August, 1914, London, HMSO, 1914

Summary of First World War Capital Court Martial Cases, Public Record Office, WO 93/49

Court of Enquiry into the Failure of a party of the 11th Border Regiment to carry out an attack on 10 July, 1916, Wellcome Institute for the History of Medicine, RAMC 446/18

'Useless Men',(1916), Wellcome Institute for the History of Medicine, RAMC 446/18

'Officers – Fitness for Duty' (1916), Wellcome Institute for History of Medicine, RAMC 446/18

Hansard, Reports of Proceeding in Parliament

205

Autobiographical fragments by Dr H.W. Hills, writtten in 1970 and
   unpublished.
Psychological Disturbances Some Suffer After Being Involved in War,
   Despatches, Channel Four Television, 27 February, 1991
Information supplied by Combat Stress, the Ex-Services Mental
   Welfare Society
The Times, News Items

Index

Mental Health Bill (1915), 54
"Mental"/"Mental?",
    classifications, 63
Mesmer, Franz Anton
    mesmerism, 29–39
    see also Hypnosis
Messines Ridge offensive (1917),
    99–100
Middle East, war in, 145
Military hospitals
    Craiglockhart, 82, 90, 109,
        111–13
    in England, 53, 55, 60, 68,
        108–09, 120
    field, 38–39, 53, 106
    forward psychiatric clearing,
        38–39, 81, 157, 164
    Second World War, 133, 157
    see also Place of treatment
Military Services Act (1916), 67
Militia, 35
Ministry of Defence, and Gulf War
    Syndrome, 177
Mitchell, Silas Weir, 19–20, 23–24
Montgomery, General Sir Bernard,
    149
Morale
    after Somme, 75, 78–79
    in French army (1917), 97–98
    in German Army, 117
    importance of, 120, 130, 150
Morality, see Character
Moran, Lord, 51, 70, 77
Morris, Charles, surgeon, 37
Moss Side Red Cross Hospital,
    Liverpool, 60, 90, 108–09
Mott, Dr Fred, Lettsomian
    lectures, 68–69
Mussolini, Benito, 144, 145, 153
Myers, Dr Charles S., 57, 119
    and causes of shell-shock, 43–44,
        81–82
    treatment methods, 52–53, 87,
        98–99

Nerve injuries, and shock, 23–24
Nervous exhaustion (neurasthenia),
    24–25, 44–46, 127, 129
Netley, Royal Victoria Hospital, 53
Neurasthenia, see Nervous
    exhaustion
Neurological boards, 120
Neurology, development of, 13, 21,
    23–28, 31
Neurosis, use of term, 24–25
Neuve Chapelle offensive (March,
    1915), 50
New York Medical Journal, 18
New Zealand, 168–69
Newbold, Henry, "Vitaï
    Lampada", 41
Neymann, Dr Clarence, 47
Nightmares, 32, 46–47, 69, 129, 156
    after Falklands, 173–74
    in shell-shock cases, 111–12, 113
    as symptom of war neurosis, 143,
        152
Nivelle, General, 89, 95, 97
Nixon, Richard, US President, 166
North Africa campaign, 145,
    149–50
    US Army in, 147, 151–52, 159
Nostalgia, 8–9, 12, 16
    in American Civil War, 14, 15–16
"NYDN" (Not Yet Diagnosed
    Nervous), classification, 63, 96,
    116

Officers
    assessment of, 43, 76–77
    predisposition to neurosis, 36, 131
Official History of British Medical
    Services during the First World
    War, 86–87, 116, 120, 121
Operation Desert Storm, 175
Owen, Wilfred, 112–13

Page, Herbert, 27

213

cause of hysterical paralysis, 45,
   59
as cause of shell-shock, 44, 64,
   73, 127, 128
and causes of windage, 17–19
Shell-shock
   causes of, 67–68, 72–73, 81–82,
      86
   Committee of Enquiry (1922),
      124–35
   grading of cases, 63, 87–88, 96,
      104, 116, 119–20
   psychological origin recognized,
      9, 87
   recognized by War Office, 46, 69,
      87, 104
   suspicion of, 104–05
   symptoms of, 46–47, 64–65,
      68–69, 82
   use of term, 43–44, 126, 127, 128
   see also Insanity; Irritable heart;
      Nostalgia; Psychiatric
      casualties; Treatment; War
      neurosis
Sherriff, R.C., 43
Ship, John, on drunkenness, 10–11
Shock, 67–68
   and nerve injuries, 23–24
   see also Commotional disorders;
      Railway spine; Windage
Shrapnel shell, 14
Sicily, invasion of, 152
"Sick", classification, 87–88, 96,
   104, 120
Singapore, fall of, 149
Slater, Eliot, 142–44
Sleep, lack of, 3, 52, 58, 82
   see also Fatigue; Insomnia
Sleeping on post, offence of, 58
Sloggett, Surgeon General Sir
   Arthur, 81
Snowden, Philip, MP, 101, 102, 114
Soldiers
   quality of conscripts, 75–76

resilience of, 36, 179
types prone to nostalgia, 15–16
see also Officers
Somme Offensive (1916), 73–74, 75,
   76, 77, 86
Southborough, Lord, and Enquiry
   into shell-shock, 124–25
Special Medical Board, for pension
   entitlements, 97
Springfield House Hospital,
   Wandsworth, 60
Stammering, 12, 69, 156
Statistics of the Military Effort . . .,
   136
Stress, 68, 90, 127
   causes of, 128–29, 142
   see also Horrors of war
Subconscious, role of, 29, 31–32
Suggestive therapy, 55, 65
Swiss, notalgia among, 8
Symptoms,
   of Gulf War Syndrome, 176–77
   of irritable heart, 16, 22–23
   of neurasthenia, 38, 40, 44–46
   of nostalgia, 8, 9, 16
   of PTSD, 168
   of railway spine, 26–27
   of shell-shock, 46–47, 64–65,
      68–69, 82–83
   of shock, 24
   of war neurosis, 142–43, 144,
      150, 152–53, 156
   see also Treatment

Taylor, A.J.P., 149
Territorial Army, 43, 49, 139
   see also Militia
Thatcher, Margaret, Prime
   Minister, 171–72
Therapy, occupational, 143, 156
Thirty Years War, "nostalgia" in, 7
Thurtle, Ernest, MP, 136–37
Tobruk, fall of, 149
Training, 130

216